Contents

Introduction to the course

Syllabus overview

This unit teaches students management accounting principles and concepts. Students will understand the nature and importance of different concepts such as cost behaviour, cost analysis, standard costing and contribution theory. They will know when each technique should be used to aid the planning and decision making of an organisation and the subsequent analysis for control purposes.

They will learn the key performance indicators that should be used to aid the performance monitoring of an organisation, and the techniques for assessing changes to an organisation (what-if analysis). The student will build a toolbox of techniques, understand the nature of the technique and when each should be used.

Test specification for this unit assessment

Assessment method	Marking type	Duration of assessment
Computer based assessment	Partially computer/ partially human marked	2.5 hours

Learning outcomes		Weighting
1	Analyse a range of costing techniques to support the management accounting function of an organisation	10%
2	Calculate and use standard costing to improve performance	40%
3	Demonstrate a range of statistical techniques to analyse business information	10%
4	Use appropriate financial and non-financial performance techniques to aid decision making	30%
5	Evaluate a range of cost management techniques to enhance value and aid decision making	10%
Total		**100%**

AAT

Final Accounts Preparation

Level 3

Course Book

For assessments from
1 September 2016

First edition June 2016

ISBN 9781 4727 4813 3
ISBN (for internal use only) 9781 4727 4869 0

British Library Cataloguing-in-Publication Data
A catalogue record for this book is available from the
British Library

Published by

BPP Learning Media Ltd
BPP House, Aldine Place
142-144 Uxbridge Road
London W12 8AA

www.bpp.com/learningmedia

Printed in the United Kingdom by Wheatons Exeter Ltd
Hennock Road
Marsh Barton
Exeter
EX2 8RP

Your learning materials, published by BPP Learning Media
Ltd, are printed on paper obtained from traceable
sustainable sources.

BPP
LEARNING MEDIA

Assessment structure

2½ hours duration

Competency is 70%

*Note that this is only a guideline as to what might come up. The format and content of each task may vary from what we have listed below.

Your assessment will consist of 10 tasks

Task	Expected content	Max marks	Chapter ref	Study complete
Task 1	**Identification of costing information** Preparation of a standard cost card or extract of information from a standard cost card or budgetary control report. Information can be given in a variety of forms for this task and students may be required to apply basic costing knowledge in order to arrive at the correct cost or quantity.	12	Cost classification and behaviour Methods of costing – activity based costing (ABC)	
Task 2	**Direct materials, labour and variable overhead variances** Calculation of direct material and direct labour standard cost variances. Students may be given a budgetary control report and asked to calculate the four material and labour variances, alternatively this task may consist of several shorter tasks, asking for the variances in turn. Tasks may also give a variance and require students to calculate one of the other variables (so called 'backward' variances). The variances required for this task are: Direct material price Direct material usage Direct labour rate Direct labour efficiency Variable overhead rate Variable overhead efficiency	16	Variance analysis	

Task	Expected content	Max marks	Chapter ref	Study complete
Task 3	**Fixed Overhead variances** Same format as task 2, except here students will be required to calculate the following four variances: Fixed overhead expenditure Fixed overhead volume Fixed overhead capacity Fixed overhead efficiency	16	Variance analysis	
Task 4	**Standard cost reporting using an operating statement.** This task provides a budgetary control report and variances and requires the completion of an operating statement reconciling the standard cost of actual production with the actual costs. Only some variances will have a sign given, identification of the rest will be required.	12	Variance analysis	
Task 5	**Statistical techniques** The following techniques could be tested in this task: Seasonal variations Moving averages Trend identification Forecasting using the identified trend and seasonal variation Index number calculations Using the regression equation	12	Forecasting data	
Task 6	**Drafting reports on variance analysis (written)** The requirement here can involve: Identifying signs for variances Explaining what they mean Suggesting reasons for each variance Explaining any links between the variances	22	Further aspects of variance analysis	

Task	Expected content	Max marks	Chapter ref	Study complete
Task 7	**Calculation of Performance indicators** Calculations are required here from budgeted financial statements, for example: Sales price per unit Material/labour/fixed production cost per unit Gross and net profit margins Return on net assets Gearing Inventory holding period It is imperative that students learn the formulae for the ratios	20	Performance indicators	
Task 8	**Decision making** This task requires students to use one or more of the key decision making topics: Break-even analysis Margin of safety Limiting factor decisions Make or buy decisions Assessment of special orders It is essential that contribution theory and cost behaviour are understood for this task.	12	Decision making techniques	
Task 9	**Cost management techniques** This tasks covers the following topics: Lifecycle costing Target costing Cost Management Techniques (including NPV)	12	Cost management	

Task	Expected content	Max marks	Chapter ref	Study complete
Task 10	**Drafting reports on key performance indicators and scenario planning (written)**	22	Performance indicators	
	This task requires students to write a report analysing information including the gross profit margin, profit margin and key changes in the business. Students may also be asked to consider the stages of the product lifecycle and comment on the cost behaviour for different stages of the cycle and how the organisation may change as the product progresses through the cycle.			
	Usually students will be provided with two scenarios where there is a difference in the two gross profit margins and asked to analyse the differences by considering the variables of sales price, sales volume, direct material, direct labour and fixed overheads.			
	The ability to understand the relationships between the variables is crucial here.			

BPP LEARNING MEDIA

Skills bank

Our experience of preparing students for this type of assessment suggests that to obtain competency, you will need to develop a number of key skills.

What do I need to know to do well in the assessment?

This Level 3 unit is about the student being able to prepare final accounts for sole traders and partnerships, and becoming aware of alternative business organisation structures.

This purpose of this unit is to provide the background knowledge and skills a student needs to be capable of drafting accounts for sole traders and partnerships and provides the background knowledge of the regulations governing company accounts. Successful students will be able to complete tasks while being aware of potential ethical issues and know how to report information effectively. Able to work with little supervision, the student should become an accomplished member of the accounting team, seeing a financial picture of the organisation as a whole.

Assumed knowledge

Final Accounts Preparation is a **mandatory** unit. It is closely linked to the Level 3 financial accounting unit *Advanced Bookkeeping*, as well as to the Level 2 units, *Bookkeeping Transactions* and *Bookkeeping Controls*. In addition, it draws on the ethical principles from the Level 3 unit *Ethics for Accountants*. On completion of this unit, students are prepared to start the Level 4 unit *Financial Statements of Limited Companies*.

It is recommended that this unit is taken after *Advanced Bookkeeping* and with or after *Ethics for Accountants*.

Assessment style

In the assessment you will complete tasks by:

1   Entering narrative by selecting from drop down menus of narrative options known as **picklists**

2   Using **drag and drop** menus to enter narrative

3   Typing in numbers, known as **gapfill** entry

4   Entering **ticks**

5   Entering **dates** by selecting from a calendar

You must familiarise yourself with the style of the online questions and the AAT software before taking the assessment. As part of your revision, login to the **AAT website** and attempt their **online practice assessments**.

Introduction to the assessment

The question practice you do will prepare you for the format of tasks you will see in the *Final Accounts Preparation* assessment. It is also useful to familiarise yourself with the introductory information you **may** be given at the start of the assessment. For example:

We have provided the following assessment to help you familiarise yourself with AAT's e-assessment environment. It is designed to demonstrate as many as possible of the question types you may find in a live assessment. It is not designed to be used on it's own to determine whether you are ready for a live assessment.

Please note that in this sample test only your responses to tasks 1–5 and 7–9 are marked.
Equivalents of tasks 6 and 10 will be human marked in the live assessment.

This assessment contains <u>10 tasks</u> and you should attempt and aim to complete EVERY task. Each task is independent. You will not need to refer to your answers to previous tasks. Read every task carefully to make sure you understand what is required.

Where the date is relevant, it is given in the task data.

Both minus signs and brackets can be used to indicate negative numbers UNLESS task instructions say otherwise.

You must use a full stop to indicate a decimal point.
For example, write 100.57 NOT 100,57 or 100 57

You may use a comma to indicate a number in the thousands, but you don't have to.
For example, 10000 and 10,000 are both OK.

Other indicators are not compatible with the computer-marked system.

Complete all 10 tasks

---

1   As you revise, use the **BPP Passcards** to consolidate your knowledge. They are a pocket-sized revision tool, perfect for packing in that last-minute revision.

2   Attempt as many tasks as possible in the **Question Bank**. There are plenty of assessment-style tasks which are excellent preparation for the real assessment.

3   Always **check** through your own answers as you will in the real assessment, before looking at the solutions in the back of the Question Bank.

Key to icons

	Key term	A key definition which is important to be aware of for the assessment
	Formula to learn	A formula you will need to learn as it will not be provided in the assessment
	Formula provided	A formula which is provided within the assessment and generally available as a pop-up on screen
	Activity	An example which allows you to apply your knowledge to the technique covered in the Course Book. The solution is provided at the end of the chapter
	Illustration	A worked example which can be used to review and see how an assessment question could be answered
	Assessment focus point	A high priority point for the assessment
	Open book reference	Where use of an open book will be allowed for the assessment
	Real life examples	A practical real life scenario

BPP
LEARNING MEDIA

AAT qualifications

The material in this book may support the following AAT qualifications:

AAT Advanced Diploma in Accounting Level 3, AAT Advanced Diploma in Accounting at SCQF Level 6 and Further Education and Training Certificate: Accounting Technician (Level 4 AATSA)

Supplements

From time to time we may need to publish supplementary materials to one of our titles. This can be for a variety of reasons, from a small change in the AAT unit guidance to new legislation coming into effect between editions.

You should check our supplements page regularly for anything that may affect your learning materials. All supplements are available free of charge on our supplements page on our website at:

www.bpp.com/learning-media/about/students

Improving material and removing errors

There is a constant need to update and enhance our study materials in line with both regulatory changes and new insights into the assessments.

From our team of authors BPP appoints, a subject expert to update and improve these materials for each new edition.

Their updated draft is subsequently technically checked by another author and from time to time non-technically checked by a proof reader.

We are very keen to remove as many numerical errors and narrative typos as we can but given the volume of detailed information being changed in a short space of time we know that a few errors will sometimes get through our net.

We apologise in advance for any inconvenience that an error might cause. We continue to look for new ways to improve these study materials and would welcome your suggestions. Please feel free to contact our AAT Head of Programme at nisarahmed@bpp.com if you have any suggestions for us.

Organisations and their financial accounts

1

Learning outcomes

1.1	Describe the types of organisation that need to prepare final accounts

- Know brief descriptions of business organisations:

  - For profit: sole traders, partnerships, limited companies, limited liability partnerships (LLPs)

  - Not for profit: charities

- The basic differences between the structure and financial characteristics of these organisations:

  - Who own the organisation/public benefit requirement

  - Who manages the organisation

  - Where responsibility for debts the organisation cannot pay lies, and the amount of exposure

  - Whether, and how, any tax is paid

- For commercial organisations, the different terms used to represent ownership in the statement of financial position (capital and equity) and amounts taken by the owners (drawings and dividends)

- For charity organisations, representation of net assets in the statement of financial position as funds of the charity

- Recognise basic advantages and disadvantages of operating as a partnership rather than a sole trader

- Recognise basic advantages and disadvantages of incorporated status.

1.2	**Recognise the regulations applying to different types of organisation**
	• Know that different regulations apply to different organisations, including awareness of relevant:
	– Partnership legislation
	– Companies legislation and accounting standards
	– Limited liability partnership legislation
	– Charity legislation, charity regulators and statements of recommended practice
	• Know that presentation of final accounts for sole traders and partnerships is not governed by statute and accounting regulations to the same extent those for limited companies are; they have no definitive format
	• Know the importance of behaving professionally, being competent and acting with due care at work
	• Know the importance of deadlines in the preparation of final accounts.
2.1	**Describe the primary users of final accounts and their needs**
	• Know the primary users of final accounts
	• The reasons why final accounts are needed by these users.
2.2	**Describe the accounting principles underlying the preparation of final accounts**
	• Be aware of the existence of a framework within which accountants work
	• Know the underlying assumptions governing financial statements: accrual basis, going concern basis
	• Know the fundamental qualitative characteristics of useful financial information
	• Know the supporting qualitative characteristics
	• Know that financial statements should be free from material misstatement
	• Recognise circumstances when a business is no longer a going concern and be aware of the effect on the value of its asset.
2.3	**Apply ethical principles when preparing final accounts**
	• Know the importance of behaving professionally and being competent
	• Know the importance of objectivity, including awareness of the potential for conflicts of interest and bias
	• Know why security and confidentiality of information must be maintained at all times

Assessment context

Questions on this area will be tested in Tasks 1 and 2 of the exam and throughout the exam in theory elements of other questions.

Qualification context

The regulatory framework of financial statements is examined throughout your AAT studies.

Business context

The preparation of accounts from different types of organisation is the main source of revenue for a lot of income for smaller accountancy practices. An understanding of the regulatory framework is essential in order to complete the relevant returns in a timely fashion.

Chapter overview

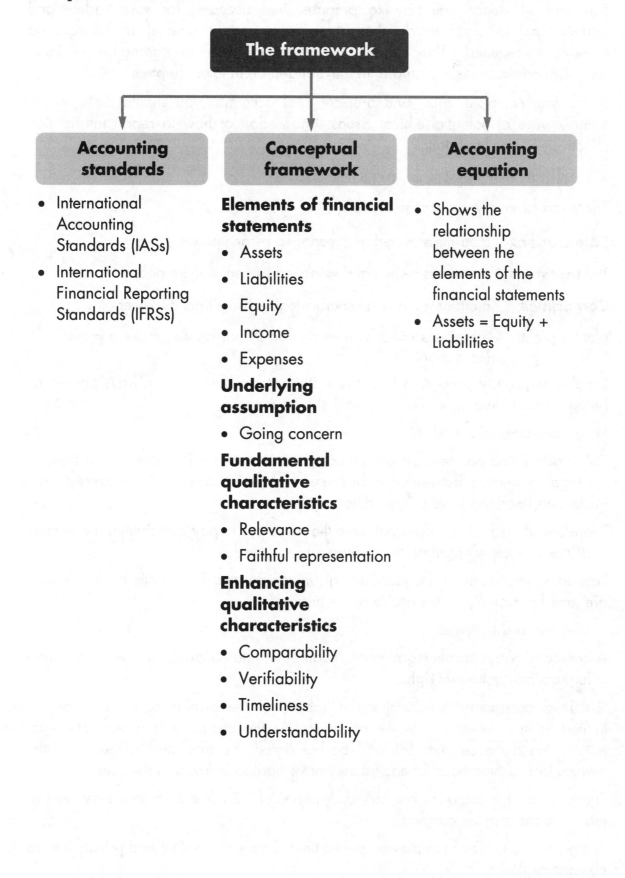

The framework

Accounting standards

- International Accounting Standards (IASs)
- International Financial Reporting Standards (IFRSs)

Conceptual framework

Elements of financial statements

- Assets
- Liabilities
- Equity
- Income
- Expenses

Underlying assumption

- Going concern

Fundamental qualitative characteristics

- Relevance
- Faithful representation

Enhancing qualitative characteristics

- Comparability
- Verifiability
- Timeliness
- Understandability

Accounting equation

- Shows the relationship between the elements of the financial statements
- Assets = Equity + Liabilities

Introduction

This unit will teach you how to prepare final accounts for sole traders and partnerships. In order to do that, there is a certain amount of background knowledge required. This chapter will introduce you to alternative business organisation structures, which are then expanded on in later chapters.

When you complete tasks, and prepare final accounts, you should do so while being aware of potential ethical issues. Knowledge of how to report information effectively is also important.

The different types of organisation

There are several types of organisation:

Sole traders: a business owned and managed by one person

Partnerships: a business owned and managed by two or more people

Companies: a business that is a separate legal **entity** from its owners

Not for profit: a business which is now conducted primarily to make a profit (eg a charity)

For the purpose of preparing financial statements, a business is always treated as being separate from its owners.

Unincorporated entities

Sole traders and partnerships are unincorporated entities. This means that there is no legal distinction between the business and their owners. Consequently, sole traders and partners have unlimited liability.

Therefore, if the business does not have the resources to pay its liabilities the owners must meet the claims against the business.

Tax does not appear in the accounts of unincorporated businesses as the owners are taxed personally on the profits of the business.

Incorporated entities

A company is a separate legal entity. It can enter into contracts, acquire assets and incur liabilities in its own right.

'Limited company' means that the liability of the owners of the company is limited to their investment in the company. As the company is a separate legal entity, should the business fail and be liquidated, the maximum amount that the owners lose is the amount of capital they have agreed to invest in the company.

The owners of a company are called shareholders. Each shareholder must own at least one share in the company.

There are two types of companies, public limited companies (Plc) and private limited companies (Ltd).

Public limited companies: may raise capital from the public on the stock exchange, although they do not have to.

Private limited companies: cannot invite the general public to invest in their shares through a stock exchange.

As companies are separate legal entities, they are taxed in their own right. Therefore, tax will appear in the financial statements of limited companies.

If the partners of a partnership don't want to be personally responsible for the business' losses, they can set up a limited partnership or limited liability partnership (LLP). LLP members are self employed for tax purposes, and the LLP itself is not taxed as a whole. The main difference between an LLP and a traditional partnership is the limited liability of each partner. The LLP is an individual person in the eyes of the law and can enter into contracts in its own name, and is therefore responsible for its own debts and liabilities. The members are only responsible for what they invest of agree to contribute towards the LLP's debts.

Owners and managers

Sole traders and partners normally own and manage their business themselves.

Limited companies (particularly the large ones) are often managed by persons other than their own.

- **Shareholders** (owners) will invest in the business but are not involved in the day to day running of the company.

- **Directors** are appointed to manage the company on behalf of the shareholders.

As shareholders are not involved in the running of the business day-to-day, they need a way of evaluating the performance of the directors. The financial statements enable them to assess the way in which the directors are safeguarding the assets of the company and using them to generate profits (stewardship of management).

To assist them in this, the components of a set of financial statements are as follows:

- Statement of financial position
- Statement of profit or loss and other comprehensive income
- Statement of changes in equity
- Statement of cash flows
- Notes to the financial statements

Required

(a)   Which of the following statements is correct?

With 'limited liability':

A company may only have a certain prescribed maximum liability on its statement of financial position	
The shareholders of a company are protected in that they can only lose their investment in the company, should the company fail	
A company can only enter into transactions involving debt up to a certain limit before gaining express approval from the shareholders in general meeting	
The shareholders may only invest in a company up to a prescribed limit per shareholder	

The following terms are used in relation to the preparation of accounts.

(i)   Statement of cash flows
(ii)   Statement of profit or loss and other comprehensive income
(iii)   Directors' report
(iv)   Statement of financial position
(v)   Statement of changes in equity
(vi)   Notes to the financial statements

(b)   A complete set of financial statements includes which of the following?

All of the above	
(i), (ii), (iii), (iv) and (v)	
(i), (ii), (iv), (v) and (vi)	
(i), (ii), (iv) and (v)	

Generally accepted accounting principles (GAAP)

Limited companies are required to observe various rules and regulations when preparing financial statements. There are established national accounting procedures which are referred to as generally accepted accounting principles (GAAP).

In most countries GAAP does not have any statutory or regulatory authority or definition, but the major components are normally:

- Accounting standards (eg International Financial Reporting Standards)

- National company law (eg Companies Act 2006 in the UK)

- Stock exchange requirements (for companies quoted on a recognised stock exchange)

Accounting standards

Recent decades have seen a dramatic rise in global trade and cross-listing on the world's capital markets. This has led to significant demand for consistent international financial information.

Organisations set up in response to this demand are:

Organisations	Standards
International Accounting Standards Committee (IASC) Founded in 1973	Issued International Accounting Standards (IAS)
International Accounting Standards Board (IASB) Formed in 2001 and replaced the IASC	Adopted existing IAS Issues International Financial Reporting Standards (IFRS)

Accounting standards state how particular transactions and events should be reflected in the financial statements.

During this course you will study a range of:

- International Accounting Standards (IAS)
- International Financial Reporting Standards (IFRS)

You do not need to learn the IAS/IFRS reference numbers for the CBT. The focus is on the practical application of the standards.

Purpose of accounting standards

The main benefits of accounting standards are credibility, discipline and comparability.

Credibility	Financial statements would lose credibility if companies carrying out similar transactions disclosed markedly different results simply because they could select accounting policies.
	Therefore, accounting standards are necessary to ensure financial reports give a true and fair view of the company.
Comparability	By having financial statements prepared on a consistent basis, inter-company comparisons can be made.

Discipline	Accounting standards detail how transactions are recognised in the financial statements, meaning there is less scope for manipulation.
	Consequently, the directors must ensure the financial statements give a true and fair view, rather than presenting the company in a favourable light.

'Principles-based' approach

IFRSs are written using a 'principles-based' approach. This means that they are written based on the definitions of the elements of the financial statements, recognition and measurement principles, as set out in the *Conceptual Framework for Financial Reporting*. This will be studied later in the chapter.

In IFRS, the underlying accounting treatments are these 'principles', which are designed to cover a wider variety of scenarios without the need for very detailed scenario by scenario guidance as far as possible.

Other GAAP, for example US GAAP, are 'rules-based', which means that accounting standards contain rules which apply to specific scenarios.

Companies Act 2006

All UK registered companies must comply with the Companies Act 2006.

The Companies Act contains many provisions relating to the formation, governance and administration of a company. For this course, you are only required to know the provisions relating to the duties and responsibilities of directors.

The Companies Act is legally binding in the UK. Therefore, contravening it is a criminal offence which may result in the directors or other responsible parties receiving penalties in the form of a fine and/or imprisonment.

Duties and responsibilities of the directors

The directors are responsible for keeping proper company accounting records.

They are also responsible for preparing the company's annual financial statements, having them audited (if the company is of a certain size) and presenting them to the shareholders in a general meeting.

The shareholders must approve the financial statements at the general meeting and then the directors are responsible for filing them with the Registrar of Companies. You may have heard this organisation referred to as Companies House.

The directors must ensure the accounts are filed with the Registrar of Companies within the prescribed period after year end.

True and fair view

The financial statements must show a true and fair view of the company's results for the period and its assets and liabilities at the end of the period.

'True and fair' is not formally defined. The concept evolves over time in accordance with changes in the business environment.

However, if financial statements are prepared in accordance with generally accepted accounting practices they will give a true and fair view (also referred to as a 'fair presentation').

Not-for-profit organisations

Not-for-profit organisations have objectives which are quite distinct in many respects.

For example:

- They do not report to shareholders (but may have stakeholders)
- Focus is often on cash flow and income generation rather than profit
- They do not normally pay dividends

Examples of not-for-profit organisations:

- Charities
- Clubs and societies
- Non-governmental organisations (NGOs).

Charities are regulated by accounting standards, charity law, relevant company law and best practice. In addition to a statement of financial position, charities produce a statement of financial activities (SOFA), an Annual Report to the Charity Commission and sometimes an income and expenditure account. The SOFA is the primary statement showing the results of the charity's activities for the period.

The Charity Commission is responsible for issuing the statement of recommended practice (SORP) for charities. The SORP for charities supplements the regular accounting standards and other legal and regulatory requirements in light of special factors relating to charities.

Activity 2: Duties and responsibilities of the directors

The following statements refer to actions that may be required in relation to companies.

(i)   Enter into contracts on behalf of the company
(ii)   File the financial statements on time
(iii)   Prepare proper accounting records
(iv)   Present the financial statements to be audited (if applicable)

Required

Which of the above statements are duties of a director?

(ii), (iii) and (iv)	
(i), (ii), (iii) and (iv)	
(i), (iii) and (iv)	
(i), (ii) and (iii)	

Limited liability partnerships (LLPs)

The Limited Liability Partnership Act 2000 (LLPA 2000) allowed the formation of a new type of legal trading entity, the Limited Liability Partnership. Despite the name, LLPs have much more in common with companies than standard partnerships.

The key features of an LLP include:

(a)   Must be registered with the Registrar of Companies, with formation documents signed by at least two members

(b)   The name of the partnership must end with LLP

(c)   Partners are known as **members**, of which there must be at least two (no upper limit applies)

(d)   The partnership **must file** annual returns and accounts; where applicable, an audit is also required

(e)   The LLP is a **separate legal entity** with all of the associated features this entails

(f)   **Members are agents** of the LLP, and can bind in the same way as partners in a standard partnership

(g)   **Members' liability is limited** to an amount stated in the partnership document (no lower limit exists)

(h)   **Designated members** are responsible for administration and filing

(i)   The LLP is not subject to **corporation tax**; the members therefore enjoy the same taxable status as partners of a standard partnership

The purpose of financial statements

The purpose of financial statements is to provide information about an organisation's:

- Financial position (assets and liabilities)
- Financial performance (profit or loss)
- Changes in financial position (cash flows)

Users need this information:

(a)   To make economic decisions (eg to assist in deciding whether to invest in the company)

(b)   To assess the stewardship of the organisation's management (how well the directors have used the company's resources to generate profit)

Activity 3: Users of the financial information

Detailed below are some of the many user groups which have an interest in financial information.

Required

What information would these users of financial information be interested in?

Solution

(a)   Managers

(b)   Employees

(c)   Investors

(d)   Lenders

(e)   Suppliers

(f)   Customers

Conceptual Framework

The *Conceptual Framework* is produced by the International Accounting Standards Board (IASB). The main objectives of this financial reporting framework is to provide the basis for:

•   The development of consistent and logical accounting standards; and
•   The use of judgement in resolving accounting issues.

(IASB, 2010)

This means that the principles of the *Conceptual Framework* are used by the IASB as a guide when producing a new accounting standard and minimise inconsistencies between them.

The *Conceptual Framework* is also used to resolve accounting issues that are not addressed directly in an accounting standard. In the absence of a standard or interpretation, management must use their judgement to determine how to account for a transaction so that the financial information remains relevant and reliable. The Framework should be used by management in exercising their judgement.

The Framework is not a financial reporting standard and as such will be overridden if there is a conflict between it and a financial reporting standard.

Qualitative characteristics of useful financial information

The qualitative characteristics of useful financial information identify the types of information that are likely to be most useful to existing and potential investors, lenders and other creditors for making decisions about the reporting entity on the basis of information in its financial report (financial information).

They are placed into two categories:

- Fundamental qualitative characteristics
- Enhancing qualitative characteristics

You have seen in your previous studies how individual transactions are first categorised in the books of prime entry, then summarised in the nominal ledger and how these balances are used to prepare the initial trial balance.

After the initial trial balance is produced some final adjustments may need to be made using the journal book and then the final financial statements can be produced.

We also saw that there are many different user groups who are interested in financial information and that, while each user group has different specific needs, all are interested in the performance, profitability and security of an individual business.

Users therefore want to be able to compare the financial information of different businesses and so it is imperative that the accounting profession has a set of common concepts on which financial information is based.

There are **four** such accounting principles: **going concern**, **accruals**, **prudence** and **consistency**.

Accounting principles

Going concern

The financial statements are normally prepared on the assumption that an entity is a going concern and will continue in operation for the foreseeable future. Hence, it is assumed that the entity has neither the intention nor the need to liquidate or curtail materially the scale of its operations; if such an intention or need exists, the financial statements may have to be prepared on a different basis and, if so, the basis used is disclosed.

Accruals

The effects of transactions and other events are **recognised when they occur**.

This means that:

- Income and expenses are recorded in the financial statements when the business has **earned the income** or **incurred the cost** rather than when cash is received or paid

- Income and costs are matched to each other so that the cost of buying something that a business later sells is shown in the same financial period as the income from the sale (again, regardless of when the cash is received or paid)

- Items are reported in the financial statements of the period to which they relate

The accruals principle is also known as the **matching** principle.

There are many adjustments made in a set of financial statements due to the accruals principle.

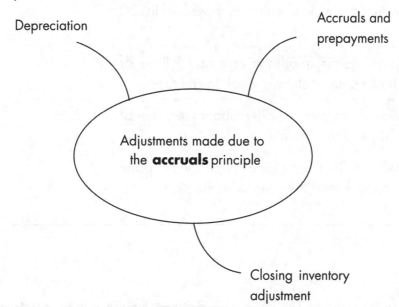

Prudence

Income and profits are **not anticipated** but are only recognised once they can be assessed with **reasonable certainty**.

Costs, losses and liabilities are recognised once you have an **obligation** in relation to them.

There are many adjustments made in a set of financial statements due to prudence.

Inventory valuation (lower of cost and net realisable value)

Adjustments made due to the principle of **prudence**

Irrecoverable and doubtful debts

Activity 4: Prudence

Required

Indicate whether it would be prudent for a business to recognise (include) the transactions below in its financial statements.

	Yes	No
A customer buys 50 litres of paint from you and you provide them with an invoice which is payable in 30 days.		
Another customer enquires about the cost of 75 litres of paint and says he'll come back next week to get them.		
You obtain a quote from your supplier about the price of stocking a new 'wipe clean' paint.		
Your supplier delivers 30 litres of the 'wipe clean' paint to you and says he will send the invoice in the post.		

Consistency

Like items are accounted for on a **consistent basis** within **each accounting period and from one period to the next**.

Accounting characteristics

The financial statements are used by a variety of stakeholders. The overriding purpose of preparing these is to **provide information**, particularly to the business owner.

This information should enable those using the final accounts to make good economic decisions, such as:

• Whether to invest more in the business
• Whether to expand and buy more non-current assets
• Whether the business could secure a bank loan to fund these purchases

If these sorts of decisions are to be made then there is a need for the financial information to possess certain **characteristics**.

These characteristics are: relevance, reliability, comparability, ease of understanding and materiality.

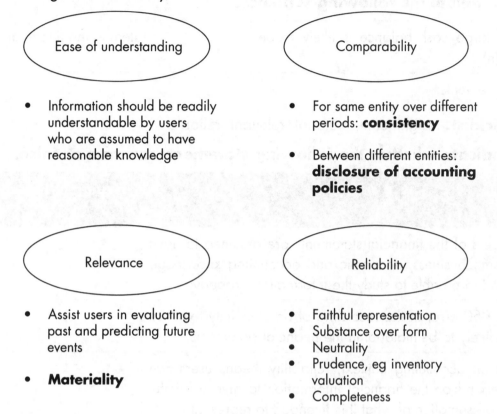

Ease of understanding

- Information should be readily understandable by users who are assumed to have reasonable knowledge

Comparability

- For same entity over different periods: **consistency**
- Between different entities: **disclosure of accounting policies**

Relevance

- Assist users in evaluating past and predicting future events
- **Materiality**

Reliability

- Faithful representation
- Substance over form
- Neutrality
- Prudence, eg inventory valuation
- Completeness

Materiality

An item is material if its **omission** or **misstatement** could reasonably influence the economic decisions taken by a user of the financial statements.

The materiality of an item should always be considered when determining whether information is relevant.

Accounting policies

An accounting policy relates to the way in which an item is treated in the financial statements. For example, inventories are valued at the lower of cost and net realisable value.

The above qualities should all be kept in mind when deciding on the most appropriate accounting policy for each item in the financial statements. For example, using the same accounting policies as those which are standard for a particular industry is likely to improve the relevance of the information provided.

Activity 5: Accounting characteristics

Required

(a) Complete the following sentence.

A large cash balance is likely to be a(n)		item in the financial
statements.		

Picklist: insignificant, material, relevant, reliable

(b) Indicate whether the following statements are true or false.

	True ✓	False ✓
Users of the financial statements are assumed to have some business, economic and accounting knowledge and to be able to study the information properly.		
A £50 error in the recording of an electricity expense is likely to be material in the financial statements.		
In an accounting context, reliability means users can depend on the financial information to give a faithful representation of what it is intended to represent.		

Activity 6: Accounts preparation – Knowledge

This task is to test your knowledge.

Required

(a) Why must like items be accounted for on a consistent basis? Choose the ONE most suitable reason.

	✓
To ensure that all items are recorded	
So that financial statements are more useful and comparable	
So that we know the company will continue in operation for the foreseeable future	
So that the company can be valued	

Income and expenses are recorded in the financial statements when the business has earned the income or incurred the cost rather than when cash is received or paid.

(b) Which principle does this reflect?

	✓
Accruals	
Consistency	
Going concern	
Prudence	

Professional ethics

Professions

A profession is an occupation that requires extensive training and the study and mastery of specialised knowledge, and usually has a professional association, ethical code and process of certification or licensing.

Codes

Professional bodies will issue **'Codes of Conduct'** or **'Codes of Ethics'**, which members are expected to adhere to. These may be developed using one of two approaches:

(a) A **rules-based approach = prescriptive**, creating specific rules for members to follow in as many situations as possible

(b) A **framework-based approach = values and qualities**, describing fundamental values and qualities that members should aspire to, but not laying out prescriptive rules.

Difference between approaches

The difference between the two approaches can be demonstrated by considering the discipline procedures for employees of most companies. Serious offences, such as violence, drinking and drug offences are always treated as gross misconduct and immediate dismissal. They are always wrong, and therefore punished. This is an example of a rules based approach. Other offences such as time keeping go through more stages and the reasons are investigated (child care issues vs lazy), discretion is then applied. Whether the offence is wrong or not depends on the circumstances and perhaps the consequences. This is an example of a framework based approach.

A code of ethics for accountants

International Ethics Standards Board

Accountancy is a high-profile profession and accountants are frequently in positions of trust and responsibility. A code of ethics for accountants has been issued by the **International Ethics Standards Board (IESBA)**, whose work is facilitated by the International Federation of Accountants (IFAC). This code has formed the basis for the AAT Code of Professional Ethics. Principles of the code include:

(a) **Integrity – acting with truthfulness and honesty**

(b) **Objectivity – reaching conclusions without undue influence or bias**

(c) Professional **competence** and due care – maintaining a high level of skill and knowledge

(d) **Confidentiality – not sharing confidential information, unless terrorism or money laundering is suspected for example**

(e) Professional **behaviour – behaving in a way that does not bring the institute into disrepute**

(AAT, 2014)

AAT students and members

To meet these principles, students and members of the AAT need to develop a mix of personal and professional qualities.

Personal qualities include:

(a) Reliability – all work must meet professional standards

(b) Responsibility – taking ownership for your work

(c) Timeliness – delays can be costly and disruptive

(d) Courtesy – to colleagues and clients

(e) Respect – to develop constructive relationships

Professional qualities include:

(a) Independence – not only being independent, but also appearing to be independent

(b) Scepticism – questioning information and data

(c) Accountability – for judgements and decisions

(d) Social responsibility – to your employer and the public

Threats to independence and conflicts of interest

The IESBA Code outlines the threats to an accountant's independence that could arise in a variety of situations. These are:

(a) **Self-interest threat**

Occurs when a firm or a member of the assurance team has some financial or other interest in an assurance client, eg providing a loan to a client

(b) **Self-review threat**

Occurs when a previous judgement needs to be re-evaluated by members responsible for that judgement, eg providing a valuation for a client's pension liability and subsequently auditing the liability

(c) **Advocacy threat**

Occurs when members promote a position or opinion to the point that subsequent objectivity may be compromised, eg acting as an advocate on behalf of an assurance client in litigation or disputes with third parties

(d) **Familiarity threat**

Occurs when, because of a close relationship, members become too sympathetic to the interests of others, eg long association with a client/boss leading to overfamiliarity with client/management such that professional judgement could be compromised

(e) **Intimidation threat**

Occurs when members are deterred from acting objectively by threats, actual or perceived, eg being pressured to reduce inappropriately the extent of work performed in order to reduce fees

(IESBA, 2015)

These threats can arise from many situations which accountants could find themselves facing. The following represent some instances of these threats in operation but is by no means an exhaustive list.

- Pressure from an overbearing colleague or from family or friends

- Members asked to act contrary to technical and/or professional standards

- Divided loyalties between colleagues and professional standards

- Publication of misleading information

- Members having to do work beyond their degree of expertise or experience they possess

- Personal relationships with other employees or clients

- Gifts and hospitality being offered

Data protection and security

There is a risk that information about individuals and companies could be misused. It is felt that an individual or company could easily be harmed by the decimation of data about the company which could be **transferred to unauthorised third parties**. This could lead to a loss of competitive advantage.

The **key risks** affecting data are:

(a) Human error
(b) Technical malfunction
(c) Deliberate/malicious action
(d) Hacking

Accountants should identify and mitigate these risks in order to protect their clients and other stakeholders.

Chapter summary

- The purpose of financial statements is to provide information about an entity's financial performance and financial position that is useful to a wide range of users for making economic decisions and assessing the stewardship of the entity's management.

- There are several broad types of organisation:

    - Profit-making

        (1) Sole traders
        (2) Partnerships
        (3) Companies

    - Not for profit

        (1) Charities, clubs and societies
        (2) Public sector organisations

- A limited company:

    - Has a separate legal personality from those of its owners
    - Gives its shareholders (owners) limited liability

- Limited liability means that the owners' liability is limited to the amount that they have paid for their shares. This is the maximum amount that they can lose if the company is wound up.

- Limited companies are owned by shareholders and managed by directors.

- Appropriate accounting policies should be chosen by considering and balancing four objectives – relevance (including materiality), reliability, comparability and ease of understanding.

- The materiality concept allows immaterial items to be treated in a manner which would not be appropriate for material items – the level of materiality will depend upon the size of the business.

- Ethics have been defined as a set of moral principles which determine our perception of right and wrong. These are distinct from the legal rules that we have to comply with.

- Professional bodies including the AAT issue codes of practice adopting a rules-based approach or a framework-based approach. The IESBA Code forms the basis of the AAT Code and it covers both principles and qualities required of members of accountancy bodies.

Keywords

- **Sole trader:** a business owned and managed by one person
- **Partnership:** a business jointly owned and managed by two or more people
- **Company:** a business that is a separate legal entity from its owners
- **Entity:** any organisation (whether profit-making or not for profit) that prepares accounts as a separate entity from its owners
- **Public limited companies:** companies that can invite members of the general public to invest in their shares
- **Private limited companies:** companies that cannot invite members of the general public to invest in their shares

Activity answers

Activity 1: Limited companies

(a)

A company may only have a certain prescribed maximum liability on its statement of financial position	
The shareholders of a company are protected in that they can only lose their investment in the company, should the company fail	✓
A company can only enter into transactions involving debt up to a certain limit before gaining express approval from the shareholders in general meeting	
The shareholders may only invest in a company up to a prescribed limit per shareholder	

(b)

All of the above	
(i), (ii), (iii), (iv) and (v)	
(i), (ii), (iv), (v) and (vi)	✓
(i), (ii), (iv) and (v)	

Activity 2: Duties and responsibilities of the directors

(ii), (iii) and (iv)	✓
(i), (ii), (iii) and (iv)	
(i), (iii) and (iv)	
(i), (ii) and (iii)	

Activity 3: Users of the financial information

(a) **Managers**

- Profitability
- Future prospects/plans to develop the business
- Current financial security
- Future financing needs/concerns
- Ability to pay a return to the owners (drawings/dividends)

(b) **Employees**

- Profitability
- Long-term growth
- Job security
- Likelihood of bonus
- Ability to pay retirement benefits/pensions

(c) **Investors**

- Profitability
- Future prospects
- Likely risk and return
- Chance of capital growth
- Ability to pay dividends

(d) **Lenders**

- Likelihood of repayment of capital amount
- Extent of other loans and the security of their debt

(e) **Suppliers**

- Likelihood of payment on time
- Likelihood of payment at all
- Whether they should continue to supply

(f) **Customers**

- Ability of entity to continue supplying
- Profitability as a measure of value for money of goods bought

Activity 4: Prudence

	Yes	No
A customer buys 50 litres of paint from you and you provide them with an invoice which is payable in 30 days.	✓	
Another customer enquires about the cost of 75 litres of paint and says he'll come back next week to get them.		✓
You obtain a quote from your supplier about the price of stocking a new 'wipe clean' paint.		✓
Your supplier delivers 30 litres of the 'wipe clean' paint to you and says he will send the invoice in the post.	✓	

Activity 5: Accounting characteristics

(a)

A large cash balance is likely to be a financial statements.	material	item in the

(b)

	True ✓	False ✓
Users of the financial statements are assumed to have some business, economic and accounting knowledge and to be able to study the information properly.	✓	
A £50 error in the recording of an electricity expense is likely to be material in the financial statements.		✓
In an accounting context, reliability means users can depend on the financial information to give a faithful representation of what it is intended to represent.	✓	

Activity 6: Accounts preparation – Knowledge

(a)

	✓
To ensure that all items are recorded	
So that financial statements are more useful and comparable	✓
So that we know the company will continue in operation for the foreseeable future	
So that the company can be valued	

(b)

	✓
Accruals	✓
Consistency	
Going concern	
Prudence	

Test your learning

1 Given below is the trial balance for a small business that is not registered for VAT. **You are required to state, in the space next to each balance, whether it is an asset, liability, income, expense or capital, and whether the balance would appear in the statement of profit or loss (P/L) or the statement of financial position (SFP).**

	Debit £	Credit £	Type of balance	P/L SFP
Sales		41,200		
Loan		1,500		
Wages	7,000			
Non-current assets	7,100			
Opening inventory	1,800			
Receivables	3,400			
Discounts received		40		
Postage	100			
Bank	300			
Capital		9,530		
Rent	500			
Purchases	30,100			
Payables		2,500		
Discounts allowed	70			
Drawings	3,000			
Electricity	800			
Telephone	600			
	54,770	54,770		

2 **Complete the following sentences:**

(a) The gross profit of a business is the profit from

(b) The total of the current assets minus the current liabilities is known as

(c) Current liabilities are

(d) Long-term liabilities are

3 **The fact that staplers for the office have been charged as an expense to profit or loss is an example of which accounting concept?**

4 **Identify and explain each of the four objectives which should be considered in selecting accounting policies.**

5 **According to the IASB's *Conceptual Framework*, which ONE of the following is a fundamental qualitative characteristic of useful financial information?**

Consistency	
Going concern	
Relevance	
Timeliness	

Incomplete records

Learning outcomes

3.1	**Recognise circumstances where there are incomplete records**
	• Know possible reasons why information may be missing
	• Know possible reasons for inconsistencies within the records themselves
	• Provide examples of the types of figures that may be missing
	• Know the importance of acting with integrity
3.2	**Prepare ledger accounts, using these to estimate missing figures**
	• How to use the content of daybooks, including sales tax
	• How to use information from the cash-book
	• How to distinguish between relevant and non-relevant data
	• How to reconstruct ledger accounts: sales and purchases ledger control accounts, sales tax control account and the bank account,
	• How to calculate and correctly label the missing figure of such reconstructed accounts
	• How to calculate opening or closing balances from information given
	• How to adjust data for sales tax, using information given
3.3	**Calculate figures using mark-up and margin**
	• Know what margin and mark-up are and the difference between them.
	• Calculate mark-up and margin
	• Use mark-up and margin to calculate missing figures
	• Use cost of goods sold to determine a missing figure
	• Adjust data for sales tax from data provided.
3.4	**Assess the reasonableness of given figures within a particular context**
	• Recognise whether a figure is reasonable in a given context
	• Explain reasons behind the difference between an actual balance and a calculation exercise professional scepticism.

Assessment context

Questions on this area will be tested in Tasks 1 and 2 of the exam. These tasks will require you to use incomplete records techniques in order to finding missing figures such as sales, purchases, closing inventories, profit and drawings.

Qualification context

Incomplete records are only examined in *Final Accounts Preparation*.

Business context

For many individuals the thrill of running their own business comes from developing and selling products or services which they are passionate about. Often, bookkeeping and double entry is not one of those things! This can mean that the accounting records a business may keep could be 'sketchy' even though keeping proper accounting records is a legal requirement! This means that businesses may call in the help of an accountant when it comes to producing their financial statements and the accountant will often need to use the information the business does have in order to generate other missing information. The preparation of accounts from incomplete records can often generate a lot of income for smaller accountancy practices.

Chapter overview

Registered business:

- Charge Sales tax on sales which is transferred to HMRC
- Claim Sales tax suffered on purchases from HMRC
- Analyse Sales tax in the books of prime entry

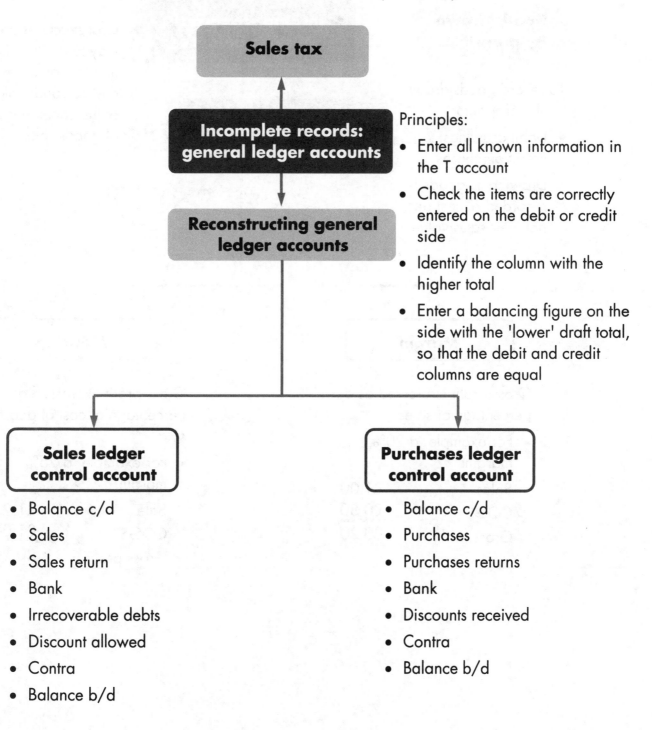

Sales tax

Incomplete records: general ledger accounts

Principles:

- Enter all known information in the T account
- Check the items are correctly entered on the debit or credit side
- Identify the column with the higher total
- Enter a balancing figure on the side with the 'lower' draft total, so that the debit and credit columns are equal

Reconstructing general ledger accounts

Sales ledger control account

- Balance c/d
- Sales
- Sales return
- Bank
- Irrecoverable debts
- Discount allowed
- Contra
- Balance b/d

Purchases ledger control account

- Balance c/d
- Purchases
- Purchases returns
- Bank
- Discounts received
- Contra
- Balance b/d

Chapter overview

- Expresses the SOFP as an equation
- Assets – Liabilities = Capital + Profit – Drawings

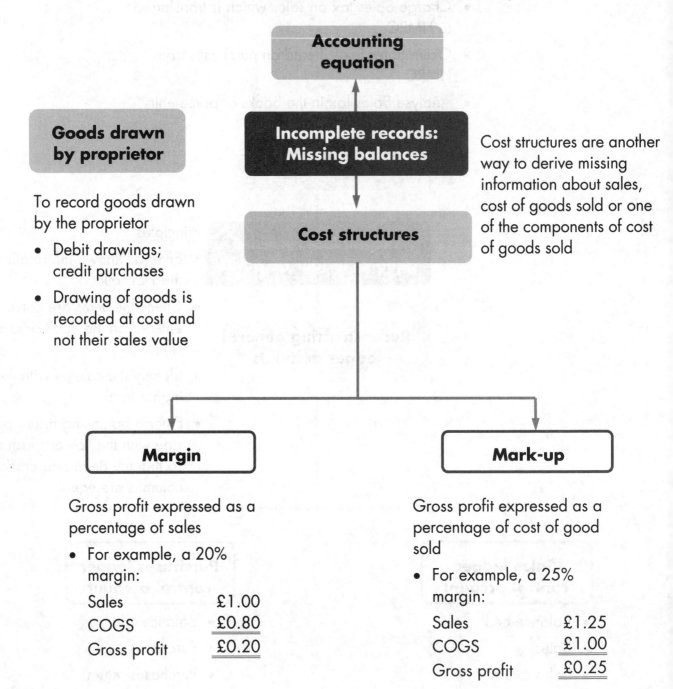

Accounting equation

Incomplete records: Missing balances

Cost structures are another way to derive missing information about sales, cost of goods sold or one of the components of cost of goods sold

Goods drawn by proprietor

To record goods drawn by the proprietor

- Debit drawings; credit purchases
- Drawing of goods is recorded at cost and not their sales value

Cost structures

Margin

Gross profit expressed as a percentage of sales

- For example, a 20% margin:

Sales	£1.00
COGS	£0.80
Gross profit	£0.20

Mark-up

Gross profit expressed as a percentage of cost of good sold

- For example, a 25% margin:

Sales	£1.25
COGS	£1.00
Gross profit	£0.25

Introduction

From our **previous** studies, we know how the 'flow of information' works for a business.

Similar transactions are **categorised** in the books of prime entry and the totals on these are then **summarised** and posted to the nominal ledger accounts.

The 'balance b/d' on each nominal ledger account is then used to extract an initial or preliminary trial balance.

The trial balance should balance, ie total debits should equal total credits! If the trial balance does balance, this minimises the possibility of errors having been made and gives the business confidence that it has processed its double entries correctly throughout the period.

However, it is still possible that the trial balance contains some errors. These are detailed below:

Type of error	Example
Error of omission	Where both sides of a transaction have been completely left out.
Error of original entry	Where an entry has been made so that debits = credits but the amount is incorrect. For example, a credit sale of £1,000 is posted as: DEBIT Sales ledger control account £150 CREDIT Sales £150
Reversal of entries	Where a transaction has been recorded at the correct amount but the debit and credit entries have been reversed. For example, posting the credit sale above as: DEBIT Sales £1,000 CREDIT Sales ledger control account £1,000
Error of principle	Here debits = credits. However, one of the entries has been made to the wrong type of account. For example, £500 spent on repairing a motor vehicle has been recorded as: DEBIT Motor vehicles at cost £500 CREDIT Bank £500 Repairs are an item of expense which should be shown in the statement of profit or loss, whereas the item has been recorded as a non-current asset.

Type of error	Example
Error of commission	Here debits = credits. However, one of the entries has been made to the wrong account, but not the wrong type of account. For example, £200 spent on telephone costs has been recorded as: DEBIT Insurance expense £200 CREDIT Bank £200 Both accounts (telephone and insurance costs) are expenses and so this is an error of commission rather than an error of principle.

If the trial balance doesn't balance, then an error has definitely been made and must be corrected.

Some of the main reasons as to why the trial balance may not balance include:

Type of error	Example
Unequal entry	Here an entry has been posted where debits ≠ credits. A common example of this is where a transposition error has been made and a figure has been reversed. For example, £450 of rent costs have been posted as follows: DEBIT Rent £450 CREDIT Bank £540 Here debits ≠ credits and so the trial balance will not balance.
One sided entry	Here a debit entry has been posted with no corresponding credit made or *vice versa*. For example, a credit sale of £300 has been posted as: DEBIT Sales ledger control account £300 or as: CREDIT Sales £300 Here debits ≠ credits and so the trial balance will not balance.

Type of error	Example
Entry duplicated on one side, nothing on the other	Here two debit entries or two credit entries have been posted. For example, the credit sale of £300 above has been posted as: DEBIT Sales ledger control account £300 DEBIT Sales £300 or as: CREDIT Sales ledger control account £300 CREDIT Sales £300 Here debits ≠ credits and so the trial balance will not balance.
Account balance incorrectly transferred to the trial balance	Here the final balance on the nominal ledger account is incorrectly transferred to the trial balance. For example, a balance of £560 on the sales account was recorded in the trial balance as £650 or £400. Note that this type of error also includes the situation where the £560 balance on the sales account was completely omitted from the trial balance. Here debits ≠ credits and so the trial balance will not balance.

A suspense account will be created and this must be cleared out when the errors are corrected via a journal entry.

As well as the correction of errors, there are other adjustments which need to be made via a journal entry before the final financial statements can be produced. These are:

- Depreciation of non-current assets
- Accruals and prepayments
- Closing inventory adjustments
- Irrecoverable and doubtful debts

These post trial balance adjustments are recorded using an **extended trial balance**.

The final figures on the trial balance are then used to produce the business's final financial statements: a statement of profit or loss and a statement of financial position.

From this process, we can see that there are several limitations of the trial balance:

- It simply lists all of the balances on the nominal ledger accounts without separating out which balances are relevant to the statement of profit or loss and which are relevant to the statement of financial position.

- It does not show a profit figure.

- It does not easily show the two elements of closing inventory: the component in the statement of profit or loss via cost of goods sold and the current asset in the statement of financial position.

Issue

Individuals running small businesses, such as a newsagent or greengrocer, may not keep all of the accounting records we have previously studied or have a detailed understanding of double entry bookkeeping. They may not have the time or resources to keep full accounting records, so instead, they just keep the basic primary records necessary to keep track of the transactions of the business.

However, they still need to know how the business is performing and need to produce financial statements. If some necessary information isn't maintained by the business, it will need to be derived from other available information. Information may also need to be derived where data has been **lost** or **stolen**.

There are several techniques available to a business to do this:

- Deriving missing figures from incomplete information (using nominal ledger accounts)

- The accounting equation

- Deriving missing figures from **cost structure** information

The skills learned in this chapter are extremely important for an accountant in practice. When reconstructing accounts, accountants must act with integrity. This means not presenting untruthful or misleading information. Therefore, the reconstruction of accounts must be done as completely and accurately as possible. Integrity is a fundamental principle of the code of professional ethics.

Sales tax (VAT): a reminder from the Level 2 accounting papers

VAT was covered in your Level 2 accounting papers and tested in those assessments. VAT does not play such an important part in the *Final Accounts Preparation* syllabus. However, questions on **incomplete records** may require knowledge of how VAT is accounted for.

A business will often need to charge VAT on the sales it makes and will also suffer VAT on its purchases. Therefore, VAT and sales tax mean the same thing for the purposes of this unit.

Provided that the business is registered for VAT, these VAT amounts do not affect the business's financial statements; it merely acts as a collecting agent for the Government.

The business charges VAT on its sales, which it passes over to the Government after deducting any VAT which it has suffered on its purchases and is therefore due back.

The VAT amounts need to be analysed separately in the books of prime entry in order for this information to be available.

A sale for £3,000 plus VAT at 20% would therefore be recorded in the sales day book as follows:

Date	Details	Net £	VAT £	Total £
16.8.X9	A Customer	3,000	600	3,600
	Total	3,000	600	3,600

It would be posted to the nominal ledger accounts using the double entry:

DEBIT	Sales ledger control account	3,600	
CREDIT	Sales		3,000
CREDIT	VAT control account		600

Similarly, a purchase for £2,000 plus VAT at 20% would be recorded in the purchases day book as follows:

Date	Details	Net £	VAT £	Total £
31.8.X9	A Supplier	2,000	400	2,400
	Total	2,000	400	2,400

It would be posted to the nominal ledger accounts using the double entry:

Account name	Debit £	Credit £
Purchases	2,000	
VAT control account	400	
Purchases ledger control account		2,400

These transactions would then be shown in the VAT control account (may also be referred to as Sales tax control account) as follows:

VAT control account

	£		£
Purchases	400	Sales	600
Balance c/d	200		
	600		600
		Balance b/d	200

The above account shows that the business owes the Government VAT of £600 in relation to sales it has made, but is due back VAT of £400 which it has suffered on its purchases.

The closing balance of £200 shows that the business has a **liability** to pay over the net VAT due.

Deriving missing figures from incomplete information

Having recapped the principles of VAT, we will see how missing figures can be derived from other available information.

Credit sales and the balance on the sales ledger control account

If the business does not keep a record of sales made on credit (ie it doesn't maintain a sales day book), this information can be derived from the opening and closing balances on the sales ledger control account (trade receivables) in conjunction with the figure for payments received.

Activity 1: Calculating sales as a missing figure

During the year ended 31 December 20X9, a business had the following balances on its sales ledger control account:

Balances as at	31 December 20X8	31 December 20X9
	£	£
Trade receivables	1,447	1,928

Payments received from credit customers during the year totalled £39,204.

Required

Find the missing sales figure by preparing the sales ledger control account for the year ended 31 December 20X9.

Solution

Sales ledger control account

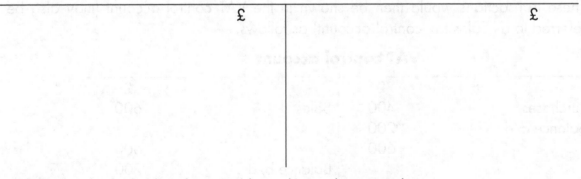

	£		£

Picklist: Balance b/d, Balance c/d, Bank, Purchases, Sales

Activity 2: Calculating contras, VAT amounts and cash balances

This task is about incomplete records and reconstructing general ledger accounts.

You are working on the accounting records of a sole trader for the year ended 30 June 20X9.

You have the following information:

Day book summaries:	Goods £	VAT £	Total £
Sales	150,000	30,000	180,000
Purchases	80,000	16,000	96,000
All sales and purchases are on credit terms			

Balances as at:	30 June 20X8 £	30 June 20X9 £
Trade receivables	22,000	47,800
Trade payables	29,500	34,600
VAT	5,780 credit	Not available
Bank	83,456 debit	Not available

Further information:	Net £	VAT £	Total £
General expenses	11,750	2,350	14,100
Purchases	80,000	16,000	96,000

Receipts and payments recorded in the bank account comprise:	£
Amounts from credit customers	140,300
Amounts to credit suppliers	88,900
Rental income	10,000
Wages	14,750
HMRC for VAT – payment	11,800
General expenses	14,100

Required

(a) Find the missing contra figure by preparing the sales ledger control account for the year ended 30 June 20X9.

Sales ledger control account

	£		£

Picklist: Balance b/d, Balance c/d, Bank, Contra, Sales day book

(b) Find the closing balance on the VAT control account for the year ended 30 June 20X9. Note. **The business is not charged VAT on its rental income.**

VAT control account

	£		£

Picklist: Balance b/d, Balance c/d, Bank, General expenses, Purchases day book, Sales day book

The totals recorded in the cash book for the year ended 30 June 20X9 were:

Receipts	£	150,300
Payments	£	129,550

(c) Assuming there are no year-end adjustments, what will be the opening balance in the cash book as at 1 July 20X9?

£		

Picklist: Debit, Credit

BPP
LEARNING MEDIA

Reminder

Note that the bank statement shows the balance from the bank's point of view, whereas the cash book is from the business's point of view.

Therefore, should a question state the bank account balance is in credit, this means that there is a **debit** balance in the business's records.

Conversely, should a question state that the bank account balance is overdrawn, then there is a **credit** balance in the business's records.

Purchases and the balance on the purchases ledger control account

A similar relationship exists between purchases of goods, the opening and closing balances on the purchases ledger control account (trade payables) and payments made to credit suppliers during the period.

Activity 3: Calculating purchases as a missing figure

During the year ended 31 March 20X9, a business had the following balances on its purchases ledger control account:

Balances as at:	31 March 20X8	31 March 20X9
	£	£
Trade payables	38,450	43,825

Payments made to credit suppliers during the year were £167,224 made from the bank account and £430 from the till.

Required

Find the missing purchases figure by preparing the purchases ledger control account for the year ended 31 March 20X9.

Solution

Purchases ledger control account

	£		£

Picklist: Balance b/d, Balance c/d, Bank, Cash, Purchases, Sales

Activity 4: Calculating missing figures in general ledger accounts

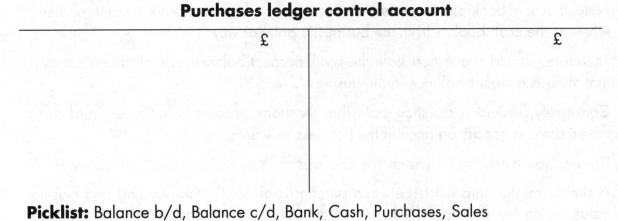

This task is about incomplete records and reconstructing general ledger accounts.

You are working on the accounts of a sole trader for the year ended 31 August 20X9.

The business is not registered for VAT.

You have the following information:

Receipts and payments recorded in the bank account include:	£
Amounts from credit customers	50,424
Amounts to credit suppliers	27,432
Interest received	180
General expenses	7,700
Purchase of a new computer	600
Cash sales banked	14,440

Balances as at:	31/08/X8 £	31/08/X9 £
Trade receivables	10,253	12,442
Trade payables	7,322	5,322
Closing inventory	9,213	7,321
Bank	923 debit	1,723 debit

You are also told that:

- All purchases of goods are on credit terms

- An irrecoverable debt for £210 was written off during the year

- An allowance for doubtful debts of £200 is to be introduced

- The proprietor draws £1,800 per month from the business bank account

- The proprietor transferred her own vehicle valued at £11,000 to the business during the year

- Computers costing over £300 are capitalised; computers costing under £300 are charged to general expenses

Required

(a) Find the credit sales figure by preparing the sales ledger control account for the year ended 31 August 20X9.

Sales ledger control account

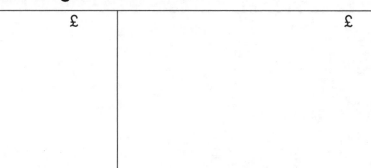

	£		£

Picklist: Allowance for doubtful debts, Allowance for doubtful debts adjustment, Balance b/d, Balance c/d, Bank, Bank charges, Cash purchases, Cash sales, Computers at cost, Credit purchases, Credit sales, Drawings, General expenses, Inventory, Irrecoverable debts, Loan

(b) **Find the amount of the loan repaid during the year by preparing a summarised bank account for the year ended 31 August 20X9.**

Bank account

	£		£

Picklist: Allowance for doubtful debts, Allowance for doubtful debts adjustment, Balance b/d, Balance c/d, Bank charges, Capital, Cash sales, Computers at cost, Drawings, General expenses, Interest received, Inventory, Irrecoverable debts, Loan, Purchases ledger control account, Sales ledger control account

The accounting equation

Statement of financial position

Statement of financial position as at 31 December 20X9

	Cost £	Accumulated depreciation £	Carrying amount £
Non-current assets			
Land and buildings	147,000	47,000	100,000
Office equipment	69,500	19,500	50,000
Motor vehicles	36,400	6,400	30,000
Furniture and fixtures	25,360	5,360	20,000
			200,000
Current assets			
Inventory	50,000		
Trade receivables	30,000		
Prepayments	3,000		
Cash and cash equivalents	7,000		
		90,000	
Total assets			290,000
Proprietor's interest			
Capital at beginning of the year	170,000		
Profit for the year	45,000		
Drawings	25,000		
		190,000	
Non-current liabilities			
Bank loans		40,000	
Current liabilities			
Bank overdraft	16,000		
Trade payables	40,000		
Accruals	4,000		
		60,000	
Total proprietor's interest and liabilities			290,000

The accounting equation expresses the statement of financial position as an equation, as the top half should come to the same total as the bottom half.

At its most simple:

Formula to learn

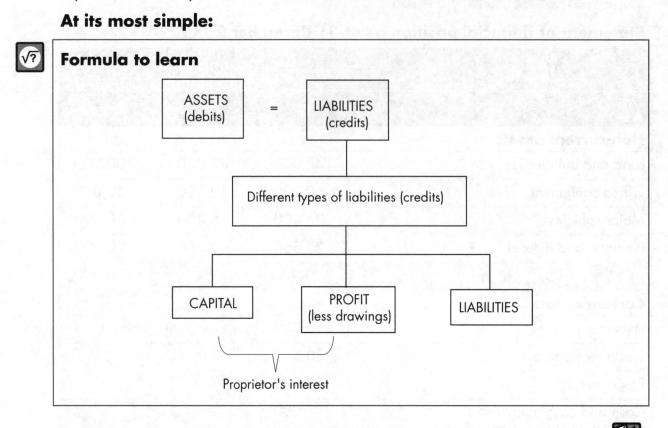

Activity 5: The accounting equation

On 1 January, the proprietor's interest in a business, Dealers, was £18,500.

At 31 January, the assets and liabilities of the business were as follows:

	£
Plant and machinery	10,000
Motor vehicles	5,000
Capital	20,500
Trade payables	3,000
Trade receivables	2,000
Drawings	1,600
Inventories	4,500
Accruals	250
Bank (debit)	3,500
Cash	250
Profit for the month	3,100

Required

(a) **What was the value of Dealers' net assets at 1 January?**

£	

(b) **Calculate the value of Dealers' assets at 31 January.**

£	

Workings

(c) **Show the accounting equation at 31 January.**

Activity 6: Missing balances and the accounting equation

This task is about calculating missing balances and the accounting equation.

You are given the following information about a sole trader as at

1 September 20X8:

- A sole trader started a business.

- The business was not registered for VAT.

- The sole trader transferred £15,000 of her own money into the business bank account.

- £600 was paid from this account for some computers.

- Goods for resale by the business costing £1,400 were purchased using the trader's personal bank account.

Required

(a) **Calculate the capital account as at 1 September 20X8, showing clearly the balance carried down.**

Capital account

	£		£
		Balance b/d	0

Picklist: Balance b/d, Balance c/d, Bank, Computers at cost, Drawings, Purchases, Purchases ledger control account, Sales, Sales ledger control account, Suspense

The following day, the trader made her first cash sale. The receipt was banked and the transaction entered in the records.

(b) **Tick the appropriate boxes to show how this transaction affects the elements of the accounting equation below.**

You must choose ONE answer for EACH row.

	Increase ✓	Decrease ✓	No change ✓
Assets			
Liabilities			
Capital			

You are given the following information about another sole trader:

- The cash book shows a debit balance of £4,250.

- The bank statement on the same date shows that the business has a credit balance of £7,500.

(c) **Which ONE of the following could explain this difference?**

	✓
Direct debits on the bank statement have not been entered in the cash book.	
Cheques to suppliers sent out at the end of the month have not yet cleared.	
A receipt from a trade receivable has been posted to the bank account in the nominal ledger twice.	

Formula to learn

Cost structures

Using a business's cost structure is another way to derive missing information about sales, cost of goods sold or one of the components of cost of goods sold (cost of sales).

Cost structure information is usually expressed in one of two ways, as either a **margin** or a **mark-up**.

(a) **Margin**: Here gross profit is expressed as a percentage of sales. For example, a margin of 25% gives:

Sales	100%
Cost of goods sold	75%
Gross profit	25%

(b) **Mark-up**: Here gross profit is expressed as a percentage of cost of goods sold. For example, a mark-up of 35% gives:

Sales	135%
Cost of goods sold	100%
Gross profit	35%

 Formula to learn

Remember that:

Cost of goods sold = opening inventory + purchases – closing inventory

Activity 7: Using margins to calculate missing balances

W Co has on average a profit margin of 40%. In 20X9, sales totalled £476,000.

Required

What is the cost of goods sold?

£	

Workings

Activity 8: Using mark-ups to calculate missing balances

Y Co operates with a standard mark-up of 30% and has the following information available for 20X9.

	£
Sales	221,000
Opening inventories	43,000
Closing inventories	47,500

Required

What is the value for purchases in 20X9?

£	

Workings

Activity 9: Calculating missing balances and the preparation of financial statements

This task is about calculating missing balances and the preparation of financial statements.

You have the following information about a sole trader:

Assets and liabilities as at 1 May 20X4	£
Plant at carrying amount	71,500
Inventory	10,000
Bank (debit balance on bank statement)	3,200
Trade payables	16,100

There were no other assets or liabilities.

Required

(a) **Calculate the following as at 1 May 20X4. Do not enter any figure as negative.**

Assets	£	
Liabilities	£	
Capital	£	

During the year ended 30 April 20X5, sales of £47,450 were made. The trader operates with a mark-up of 30%.

(b) **Calculate the cost of goods sold for the year ended 30 April 20X5.**

£	

Purchases for the year were £48,500.

(c) **Calculate the value of closing inventory.**

£	

The trader now tells you that during the year he has taken some goods for personal use.

(d) Complete the following statement:

This means that the inventory figures in the financial statements at 30 April 20X5 will be	
	the figure calculated in (c) above.

Picklist: greater than, less than, the same as

(e) Which of the following is best described as a current asset? Choose ONE answer.

	✓
A bank overdraft	
Drawings that the owner has taken during the year	
Monies owed from a credit customer	
Monies owed to a credit supplier	

Goods drawn by proprietor

Often the owner will withdraw cash from the business for their own personal use. This needs to be recorded in the accounting records and is entered via the journal:

Account name	Debit £	Credit £
Drawings (SOFP)	X	
Cash (SOFP)		X

An owner may also take goods for their own use from the business. These are also drawings but are recorded as follows:

Account name	Debit £	Credit £
Drawings (SOFP)	X	
Purchases (SPL)		X

Drawings of goods are recorded at the **cost** to the business and not at their sales value.

They are taken out of purchases and **not** recorded against inventories.

In incomplete records questions, you must ensure that all drawings are included, whether they are in the form of cash or goods.

Illustration 1: Drawings

During the year ended 31 December 20X9, Peter Albert, a sole trader, carried out the following transactions:

	£
Sales (40 units @ £100)	4,000
Purchases (45 units @ £60)	2,700
His inventory (at cost) was:	
1 January 20X9 (5 units @ £60)	300
31 December 20X9 (8 units @ £60)	480

During the year, he had withdrawn two units for his own use.

Firstly, **ignoring the drawings**, an outline trading account would appear as follows:

		£
Sales		4,000
Cost of goods sold		
Opening inventory	300	
Purchases	2,700	
	3,000	
Less closing inventory	(480)	
		2,520
Gross profit		1,480

How should the drawings of goods be treated?

The debit entry will be to **drawings** on the statement of financial position, but what about the credit entry?

It will **not** go to inventory (because these goods were not in hand at the year end so they are not included in the value of £480) but rather the adjustment will go to the **purchases account** (as this is where they will have been previously recorded).

In the trading account, this credit entry is often shown as a separate deduction from cost of goods sold (or cost of sales). For example:

	£	£
Sales		4,000
Cost of goods sold		
Opening inventory	300	
Purchases	2,700	
Less goods drawn by proprietor		
2 units @ £60	(120)	
	2,880	
Less closing inventory	(480)	
		2,400
Gross profit		1,600

Points to note

(a) Drawings of goods are recorded at **cost**.
(b) Gross profit figure now makes sense, ie profit of £40 per unit × 40 units sold.

Double entry summary for the chapter

Adjustment to record cash drawings:

Account name	Debit £	Credit £
Drawings (SOFP)	X	
Cash (SOFP)		X

Adjustment to record drawings of goods:

Account name	Debit £	Credit £
Drawings (SOFP)	X	
Purchases (SPL)		X

Chapter summary

- Many small businesses do not keep full accounting records – they have what is known as incomplete records.

- There are several techniques that can be used to piece together the information required for a statement of profit or loss and statement of financial position, even if the accounting records are incomplete.

- The opening capital balance can be found by applying the accounting equation: assets – liabilities = capital.

- The accounting equation can also be expressed as:

  increase in net assets = capital introduced + profit – drawings

  This can be used to find a missing figure such as profit or drawings.

- The three-column cash and bank account can be reconstructed, then balanced to find a missing figure such as drawings for the period.

- Receivables and payables accounts can also be reconstructed to find missing figures. There are four main entries in these accounts – opening balance, closing balance, cash received/paid, and sales/purchases – if three of the figures are known, then the fourth can be found by balancing the account.

- Mark-ups and margins for a shop require us to set up the cost structure – this can then be used to find sales if cost of sales is known, or to find cost of sales if sales are known.

- All of the techniques covered may be required in an assessment – a clear, logical approach is required, together with plenty of practice of incomplete records problems.

- The cost structure and the trading account can also be used to find the value of any missing inventory at the end of the accounting period.

Keywords

- **Incomplete records:** accounting records which are not a full set of primary records and ledger accounts

- **Net assets:** total of the assets of a business minus the liabilities

- **Mark-up:** the percentage added to cost of goods to arrive at their selling price

- **Cost structure:** the relationship in percentage terms between sales, cost of sales and gross profit

- **Margin:** gross profit expressed as a percentage of sales

Activity answers

Activity 1: Calculating sales as a missing figure

Sales ledger control account

	£		£
Balance b/d	1,447	Bank	39,204
Sales (β)	39,685	Balance c/d	1,928
	41,132		41,132

Activity 2: Calculating contras, VAT amounts and cash balances

(a)

Sales ledger control account

	£		£
Balance b/d	22,000	Contra (β)	13,900
Sales day book	180,000	Bank	140,300
		Balance c/d	47,800
	202,000		202,000

(b)

VAT control account

	£		£
Purchases day book	16,000	Balance b/d	5,780
General expenses	2,350	Sales day book	30,000
Bank	11,800		
Balance c/d (β)	5,630		
	35,780		35,780

(c)

£	104,206	debit

Working

£83,456 + £150,300 – £129,550

Activity 3: Calculating purchases as a missing figure

Purchases ledger control account

	£		£
Bank	167,224	Balance b/d	38,450
Cash	430	Purchases (β)	173,029
Balance c/d	43,825		
	211,479		211,479

Activity 4: Calculating missing figures in general ledger accounts

(a)

Sales ledger control account

	£		£
Balance b/d	10,253	Bank	50,424
Credit sales (β)	52,823	Irrecoverable debts	210
		Balance c/d	12,442
	63,076		63,076

(b)

Bank account

	£		£
Balance b/d	923	Purchases ledger control account	27,432
Cash sales	14,440	General expenses	7,700
Interest received	180	Computers at cost	600
Sales ledger control account	50,424	Loan (β)	6,912
		Drawings (1,800 × 12)	21,600
		Balance c/d	1,723
	65,967		65,967

Activity 5: The accounting equation

(a)

£	18,500

Assets = proprietor's interest + liabilities

Assets – liabilities = proprietor's interest

Net assets = proprietor's interest

(b)

£	25,250

Workings

	£
Plant and machinery	10,000
Motor vehicles	5,000
Trade receivables	2,000
Inventories	4,500
Bank	3,500
Cash	250
Total	25,250

(c)

Assets =	Capital	+ Profit	– Drawings	+ Liabilities
10,000 + 5,000 + 2,000 + 4,500 + 3,500 + 250 =	20,500	+ 3,100	– 1,600	+ 3,000 + 250
25,250 =	20,500	+ 3,100	– 1,600	+ 3,250

Activity 6: Missing balances and the accounting equation

(a)

Capital

	£		£
Balance c/d	16,400	Balance b/d	0
		Bank	15,000
		Purchases	1,400
	16,400		16,400

(b)

	Increase ✓	Decrease ✓	No change ✓
Assets	✓		
Liabilities			✓
Capital	✓		

(c)

	✓
Direct debits on the bank statement have not been entered in the cash book.	
Cheques to suppliers sent out at the end of the month have not yet cleared.	✓
A receipt from a trade receivable has been posted to the bank account in the nominal ledger twice.	

Activity 7: Using margins to calculate missing balances

£	285,600

Workings

Sales	= 100%	476,000	$476,000 / 100 \times 60$
COGS	= 60%	285,600	
Gross profit	= 40%	190,400	

Activity 8: Using mark-ups to calculate missing balances

£	174,500

Workings

Sales	= 130%	221,000	$221,000 / 130 \times 100$
COGS	= 100%	170,000	
Gross profit	= 30%	51,000	

Cost of goods sold	
Opening inventory	43,000
+ purchases (β)	174,500
– closing inventory	(47,500)
	170,000

Activity 9: Calculating missing balances and the preparation of financial statements

(a)

Assets	£	81,500
Liabilities	£	19,300
Capital	£	62,200

(b)

£	36,500

Working $47,450 / 130 \times 100$

(c)

£	22,000

Working

Cost of goods sold

Opening inventory	10,000
+ purchases	48,500
– closing inventory (β)	(22,000)
	36,500

(d)

This means that the inventory figures in the financial statements at 30 April 20X5 will be	
less than	the figure calculated in (c) above.

(e)

	✓
A bank overdraft	
Drawings that the owner has taken during the year	
Monies owed from a credit customer	✓
Monies owed to a credit supplier	

Test your learning

1   A business has made a profit for the year of £17,800. The opening net assets were £58,900 and the closing net assets were £71,400. The owner had paid in an additional £10,000 of capital during the year.

What were the drawings during the year?

£ [   ]

2   A business had payables on 30 April 20X9 of £4,700 and on 1 May 20X8 of £3,800. During the year payments were made to payables of £56,900 and settlement discounts were received of £1,300.

What were the purchases for the year?

£ [   ]

3   At 1 April 20X8, a business's bank statement showed a credit balance of £1,020. During the year, takings of £48,700 were paid into the bank account and payments for purchases were made of £24,600 and for expenses of £12,500. The closing bank balance was £890.

What were the owner's drawings out of the bank account for the year ending 31 March 20X9?

£ [   ]

4   A business sells its goods at a mark-up of 45% on cost. The sales for the year were £184,150.

What was the cost of sales for the year?

£ [   ]

5   A business operates with a margin of 35%. The cost of sales during the year was £130,000.

What were the sales for the year?

£ [   ]

6   A small business has asked you to help in the preparation of a statement of profit or loss and statement of financial position for the year ended 31 March 20X9. A summary of the bank statements for the year is given below:

	£
Receipts from receivables	108,500
Payments to payables for purchases	74,400
Payments for expenses	12,600

You are also given the opening and closing figures for the assets and liabilities. However, the owner does not know what the closing receivables figure is.

	1 April 20X8 £	31 March 20X9 £
Bank	430	7,200
Inventory	7,600	6,100
Receivables	10,400	not known
Payables	6,200	8,300
Accruals of expenses	800	600

The business also has non-current assets with a carrying amount of £12,600 at 1 April 20X8. It has been decided that £1,600 of depreciation should be charged for the year to 31 March 20X9.

The sales are made at a mark-up of 40%.

Prepare the statement of profit or loss and statement of financial position for the business for the year ended 31 March 20X9.

7   A business has had its entire closing inventory destroyed by a flood at the end of the year and needs a valuation in order to put in an insurance claim. The information that is known about the business's transactions for the year is:

Sales	£240,000
Purchases	£162,000
Opening inventory	£12,000
Margin	30%

What is the value of the closing inventory that was destroyed?

£ [   ]

Accounts for sole traders

Learning outcomes

4.1	Calculate opening and/or closing capital for a sole trader
	• Account for drawings, capital injections and profits or losses
	• Record these in ledger accounts
	• Explain movements in capital balances
4.2	**Describe the components of a set of final accounts for a sole trader**
	• The purpose of a statement of profit or loss
	• The purpose of a statement of financial position
	• How the statement of financial position is linked to the accounting equation
	• How the statement of profit or loss and the statement of financial position are related
4.3	**Prepare a statement of profit or loss for a sole trader in the given format**
	• Itemise income and expenditure in line with given organisational policies
	• Transfer data from the trial balance to the appropriate line of the statement according to the level of detail given for the organisation
4.4	**Prepare a statement of profit or loss for a sole trader in the given format**
	• Apply the net assets presentation of the statement of financial position
	• Transfer data from the trial balance to the appropriate line of the statement according to the level of detail given for the organisation

Assessment context

Questions on this chapter will be tested in Task 3 of the exam. This task is likely to present you with an adjusted trial balance (which balances) and you will be required to draw up a statement of profit or loss and/or a statement of financial position using the skeleton proformas provided.

Qualification context

This area completes your studies in relation to producing the final accounts for a sole trader. The concepts and principles, however, are further developed in the next chapter on partnerships, and in the preparation of the financial statements of limited companies which is examined in the Level 4 paper *Financial Statements of Limited Companies*.

Business context

All businesses need to produce financial information so that the owners know how the business has performed over a period of time. For many, this will involve the production of the statement of profit or loss and statement of financial position. The statement of profit or loss is also often used by a business to prepare information for the tax authorities.

Chapter overview

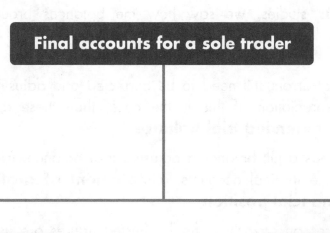

Final accounts for a sole trader

Statement of profit or loss

- Shows the income and expenses of the business for a period of time

Statement of financial position

- Shows the assets and liabilities of the business at a point in time

Introduction

In your **previous** studies, we saw how the balances brought down on the individual nominal ledger accounts are used to extract an initial or preliminary trial balance.

It may well be that errors still need to be corrected and adjustments recorded for items such as depreciation. If this is the case, then these adjustments will be recorded using an **extended trial balance**.

Once a business has a full balancing adjusted trial balance, it will then use these numbers to produce its final accounts: a **statement of profit or loss** and a **statement of financial position**.

This chapter focuses on how these final adjusted figures are used to prepare the final accounts.

Proforma financial statements

Statement of profit or loss

Statement of profit or loss for the year ended 31 December 20X9

	£	£
Sales revenue		200,000
Opening inventory	40,000	
Purchases	110,000	
Carriage inwards	20,000	
Closing inventory	(50,000)	
Cost of goods sold		120,000
Gross profit		80,000
Add:		
Interest received		5,000
Discounts received		3,000
Less:		
Rent	11,000	
Carriage outwards	4,000	
Telephone	1,000	
Electricity	2,000	

	£	£
Wages and salaries	9,000	
Depreciation charges	7,000	
Irrecoverable and doubtful debts	3,000	
Motor expenses	5,000	
Discounts allowable	1,000	
Total expenses		43,000
Profit for the year		45,000

CBT information

Note that in the CBT, accounts such as discounts received and interest received should be treated as separate additions to **gross profit**, rather than shown as a 'negative expense'.

The proformas will be set out in a format which enables you to position these items correctly.

Statement of financial position

Statement of financial position as at 31 December 20X9

	Cost £	Accumulated depreciation £	Carrying amount £
Non-current assets			
Land and buildings	160,000	60,000	100,000
Office equipment	70,000	20,000	50,000
Motor vehicles	35,000	5,000	30,000
Development costs	23,000	3,000	20,000
	288,000	88,000	200,000
Current assets			
Inventory	50,000		
Trade receivables	30,000		
Prepayments	3,000		
Cash and cash equivalents	7,000		
		90,000	

	Cost £	Accumulated depreciation £	Carrying amount £
Current liabilities			
Bank overdraft	16,000		
Trade payables	40,000		
Accruals	4,000		
		60,000	
Net current assets			30,000
Non-current liabilities			
Bank loans			40,000
Net assets			190,000
Financed by:			
Capital			170,000
Profit for the year			45,000
Drawings			(25,000)
			190,000

Points to note

Term	Consideration
Accounting equation	The statement of financial position falls naturally into two parts which are the two sides of the accounting equation – 'assets minus liabilities' and 'capital'. (Under International Accounting Standards it can be presented in a different format, with assets in the top half and capital plus liabilities in the bottom half.)
Non-current assets	These relate to assets held and used in the business over the long term (ie more than one year). There are two main types of non-current assets: • Property, plant and equipment – assets which have a physical substance, for example buildings, motor vehicles and machinery • Intangible assets – assets which do not have a physical substance, for example goodwill, brands and patents
Current assets	These relate to assets used by the business on a day to day basis and include inventories, trade receivables and bank/cash balances.

Term	Consideration
Current liabilities	These relate to liabilities owed by the business due to its day to day activities and include trade payables, accruals and bank overdrafts.
	Note that where a business is registered for VAT, it acts as a collecting agent for the Government and so the balance on the VAT control account is often a current liability because businesses tend to sell items for more than they cost, and so the VAT owed on sales will be higher than the VAT due back on purchases.
Non-current liabilities	These relate to the long-term debts of the business and include items such as long-term bank loans. The total for non-current liabilities is deducted from the total of non-current assets and net current assets to give the statement of financial position total. In terms of the accounting equation this is the total of the assets minus liabilities; that is, the business's **net assets**.
Capital	The capital or proprietor's interest section of the statement of financial position shows what the business owes back to its owner. This includes the capital contributed to date, plus the profits for the year, less any drawings taken.

CBT tasks

CBT tasks in this chapter may test your understanding of the components of the final accounts. You are also likely to be asked to prepare a statement of profit or loss and/or a statement of financial position from the adjusted balances on a trial balance.

The *Final Accounts Preparation* syllabus states that when you are asked to produce the final accounts above, you will be given a **'full balancing adjusted trial balance'**.

This means that the trial balance you are provided with will already have had any suspense account cleared and any other journal adjustments will also have been made. These would typically be for depreciation, irrecoverable debts, accruals and prepayments and so forth.

A skeleton proforma will be provided.

The activity below gives you the opportunity to practise the skills you will need in the exam.

Activity 1: Preparing final accounts for a sole trader

This task is about preparing financial statements for sole traders.

You have the following trial balance for a sole trader known as Pearl Trading. All the necessary year-end adjustments have been made.

The following are accounting policies used by Pearl Trading:

- Sales revenue should include sales returns, if any.
- Purchases should include purchases returns and carriage inwards, if any.

Required

(a) Calculate the sales revenue figure to be included in the statement of profit or loss for Pearl Trading.

£

(b) Calculate the purchases figure to be included in the statement of profit or loss for Pearl Trading.

£

(c) Prepare a statement of profit or loss for Pearl Trading for the year ended 31 August 20X9.

If necessary, use a minus sign to indicate ONLY the following:

- **The deduction of an account balance used to make up cost of goods sold**
- **A loss for the year**

Pearl Trading

Trial balance for the year ended 31 August 20X9

	Debit £	Credit £
Accruals		5,310
Bank	5,034	
Capital		20,000
Carriage inwards	4,345	
Carriage outwards	6,421	
Closing inventory	26,424	26,424
Depreciation charges	9,524	
Disposal of non-current asset		510

	Debit £	Credit £
Drawings	16,000	
General expenses	9,521	
Machinery at cost	20,000	
Machinery accumulated		8,321
Opening inventory	18,311	
Prepayments	780	
Purchases	180,130	
Purchases ledger control account		30,300
Sales		270,314
Sales ledger control account	38,310	
Sales returns	9,020	
VAT		22,952
Wages	40,311	
Total	**384,131**	**384,131**

Pearl Trading

Statement of profit or loss for the year ended 31 August 20X9

	£	£
Sales revenue		
Cost of goods sold		
Gross profit		
Add:		

	£	£
Less:		
Total expenses		
Profit/loss for the year		

Picklist: Accruals, Capital, Carriage outwards, Cash and cash equivalents, Closing inventory, Depreciation charges, Disposal of non-current asset, Drawings, General expenses, Loss, Machinery, Opening inventory, Prepayments, Profit for the year, Purchases, Sales, Trade payables, Trade receivables, VAT, Wages

(d) **Prepare a statement of financial position for Pearl Trading for the year ended 31 August 20X9. If necessary, use a minus sign to indicate drawings.**

Pearl Trading

Statement of financial position as at 31 August 20X9

	Cost £	Accumulated depreciation £	Carrying amount £
Non-current assets			
Current assets			

	Cost £	Accumulated depreciation £	Carrying amount £
Current liabilities			
Net current assets			
Net assets			
Financed by:			

Picklist: Accruals, Capital, Carriage outwards, Cash and cash equivalents, Depreciation charges, Disposal of non-current asset, Drawings, General expenses, Inventory, Loss, Machinery, Prepayments, Profit for the year, Purchases, Sales, Trade payables, Trade receivables, VAT, Wages

(e) **Identify ONE valid reason for producing an initial trial balance.**

	✓
It shows whether the business has made a profit or a loss for the period.	
It proves that double entry has taken place.	
It shows which items belong in the statement of profit or loss and statement of financial position.	
It is produced automatically by a computerised accounting system.	

You are preparing the financial statements for an organisation when you notice the following inconsistency in the books and records:

- The cost of computers in the initial trial balance shows a debit balance of £41,000.

- The total cost of the computers from a list of those present at the year end was £55,000.

(f)   Which ONE of the following could explain this difference?

	✓
A newly purchased computer was not included in the physical count.	
The theft of a computer has not been recorded in the non-current assets register.	
The sale of a computer has been omitted from the initial trial balance.	
The purchase of a computer has not been posted to the general ledger.	

Cost of goods sold and inventory in the trial balance

In the example above, the components of cost of goods sold and inventory were presented on several lines of the trial balance. Therefore, the trial balance identifies:

- Opening inventory
- Purchases
- Carriage inwards
- Closing inventory

Closing inventory is shown on the debit side (being an asset in the statement of financial position at the year end) and also on the credit side (being a reduction in cost of goods sold transferred to the statement of profit or loss at the end of the period).

All other cost of goods sold items are debit balances, as they form part of the expense transferred to the statement of profit or loss at the end of the period.

Alternative presentation of cost of goods sold and inventory

You may also see cost of goods sold and inventory shown on two lines in the trial balance. Under this presentation they would appear as follows:

Pearl Trading

Trial balance for the year ended 31 August 20X9

	Debit £	Credit £
Closing inventory	26,424	
Cost of goods sold	176,362	

Here, the statement of profit or loss balances (opening inventory, purchases, carriage inwards and closing of inventory) have been totalled and shown on the cost of goods sold line.

Closing inventory is shown on a separate line and represents the asset listed in the statement of financial position at the year end.

An example of this alternative presentation will be studied further in the chapter *Accounts for Partnerships*.

Chapter summary

- Debit balances in the trial balance will be expenses, assets or drawings.

- Credit balances in the trial balance will be income, liabilities or capital.

- The opening inventory figure in the trial balance is an expense.

- The closing inventory figures in the trial balance are:

    - An asset; and
    - A reduction in an expense.

- The statement of profit or loss is a historical summary of the activities of the business during the accounting period. It shows the income of the business minus the expenses.

- Discounts allowed are expenses deducted to arrive at profit for the year. Discounts received should be shown as income just below gross profit.

- The statement of financial position is a 'snapshot' of the business on the last day of the accounting period listing all of the assets, liabilities and capital of the business.

- The statement of financial position is a vertical form of the accounting equation showing that the assets minus the liabilities (net assets) equal the capital balance.

- Assets are listed in a particular order starting with non-current assets and followed by current assets. The current assets are listed in a particular order starting with the least liquid, inventory, and working down to the most liquid, bank and cash balances.

- Current liabilities are the payables of the business that are due to be paid in less than 12 months' time – current liabilities are deducted from the total of the current assets to give a figure known as net current assets.

- Non-current liabilities payable after more than 12 months are deducted from the total of the non-current assets and net current assets, to give the final statement of financial position total (net assets).

- Capital is made up of the opening balance of capital plus the profit for the year from the statement of profit or loss less the owner's drawings. This calculation should give the statement of financial position total, that is capital = net assets (assets less liabilities).

- Income and expense ledger accounts are cleared to the profit or loss ledger account at the end of the accounting period, leaving no remaining balance on these accounts.

- The statement of financial position ledger accounts – asset, liability and capital account balances – on the last day of the accounting period remain in the ledger accounts to become the opening balances at the start of the next accounting period.

Keywords

- **Statement of profit or loss:** one of the main financial statements showing the income of the business less the expenses of the business for the last accounting period

- **Gross profit:** the profit earned by the business from its trading activities – shown in the trading account

- **Profit for the year:** the final profit of the business after all expenses have been deducted

- **Statement of financial position:** a list of all the assets, liabilities and capital of the business on the last day of the accounting period

- **Current assets:** the short-term assets of the business – inventory, receivables and cash and bank balances

- **Current liabilities:** liabilities that are due to be paid within one year of the statement of financial position date

- **Net assets:** total assets less total liabilities

- **Net current assets:** the total of the current assets minus the current liabilities

- **Non-current liabilities:** liabilities that are due to be paid more than a year after the statement of financial position date

Activity 1: Preparing final accounts for a sole trader

(a)

£	261,294

Tutorial working: 270,314 – 9,020 = 261,294

(b)

£	184,475

Tutorial working: 180,130 + 4,345 = 184,475

(c)

Pearl Trading
Statement of profit or loss for the year ended 31 August 20X9

	£	£
Sales revenue		261,294
Opening inventory	18,311	
Purchases	184,475	
Closing inventory	–26,424	
Cost of goods sold	176,362	
Gross profit		84,932
Add:		
Disposal of non-current asset		510
Less:		
Carriage outwards	6,421	
Depreciation charges	9,524	
Wages	40,311	
General expenses	9,521	
Total expenses		65,777
Profit/loss for the year		19,665

(d)

Pearl Trading
Statement of financial position as at 31 August 20X9

	Cost £	Accumulated depreciation £	Carrying amount £
Non-current assets			
Machinery	20,000	8,321	11,679
Current assets			
Inventory	26,424		
Trade receivables	38,310		
Prepayments	780		
Cash and cash equivalents	5,034		
		70,548	
Current liabilities			
Trade payables	30,300		
Accruals	5,310		
VAT	22,952		
		58,562	
Net current assets			11,986
Net assets			23,665
Financed by:			
Capital			20,000
Profit for the year			19,665
Drawings			(16,000)
			23,665

(e)

	✓
It shows whether the business has made a profit or a loss for the period.	
It proves that double entry has taken place.	✓
It shows which items belong in the statement of profit or loss and statement of financial position.	
It is produced automatically by a computerised accounting system.	

(f)

	✓
A newly purchased computer was not included in the physical count.	
The theft of a computer has not been recorded in the non-current assets register.	
The sale of a computer has been omitted from the initial trial balance.	
The purchase of a computer has not been posted to the general ledger.	✓

Test your learning

1 A sole trader had a balance on her capital account of £34,560 on 1 July 20X7. During the year ending 30 June 20X8, she made a net profit of £48,752 but withdrew £49,860 from the business.

What is the capital balance at 30 June 20X8?

£ [   ]

2 The owner of a business took goods from inventory for his own use which had originally cost £1,500 and which had a selling price of £2,100.

What are the two alternative double entry accounting treatments for this transaction?

(a) DEBIT [   ]

CREDIT [   ]

(b) DEBIT [   ]

CREDIT [   ]

3 The telephone expense and insurance expense accounts of a sole trader have balances of £3,400 and £1,600 respectively at 30 September 20X8. However, £300 of telephone expense is to be accrued and £200 of insurance has been prepaid.

What are the final expense figures that will appear in the statement of profit or loss for the year?

Telephone expense   £

Insurance expense   £

4 A sole trader has the following balances in her initial trial balance at 31 May 20X8:

	£
Furniture and fittings at cost	12,600
Motor vehicles at cost	38,500
Accumulated depreciation at 1 June 20X7:	
Furniture and fittings	3,400
Motor vehicles	15,500

Furniture and fittings are depreciated at the rate of 20% per annum on cost, and motor vehicles are depreciated on the reducing balance basis at a rate of 30%.

Complete the table below to show the total carrying amount of the non-current assets that will appear in the statement of financial position at 31 May 20X8.

Non-current assets

	Cost £	Accumulated depreciation £	Carrying amount £
Furniture and fittings			
Motor vehicles			

5 Given below is the list of balances taken from a sole trader's ledger accounts at 30 June 20X8.

	£
Sales	308,000
Machinery at cost	67,400
Office equipment at cost	5,600
Office costs	2,300
Distribution costs	4,100
Sales ledger control	38,400
Telephone expenses	1,800
Purchases ledger control	32,100
Heat and light	3,100
Bank overdraft	3,600
Purchases	196,000
Petty cash	100
Insurance	4,200
Accumulated depreciation – machinery	31,200
Accumulated depreciation – office equipment	3,300
Inventory at 1 July 20X7	16,500
Loan from bank	10,000
Miscellaneous expenses	2,200
Wages	86,700

	£
Loan interest	600
Capital	60,000
Drawings	20,000
Allowance for doubtful debts	1,000

The following information is also available:

(i) After drawing up the initial trial balance, the bookkeeper spotted that the heat and light account had been undercast by £200.

(ii) The value of inventory at 30 June 20X8 was £18,000.

(iii) The machinery and office equipment have yet to be depreciated for the year. Machinery is depreciated at 30% on the reducing balance basis; and office equipment, at 20% of cost.

(iv) £200 of loan interest has yet to be paid for the year and a telephone bill for £400 for the 3 months to 30 June 20X8 did not arrive until after the trial balance had been drawn up.

(v) Of the insurance payments, £800 is for the year ending 30 September 20X8.

(vi) An irrecoverable debt of £1,200 is to be written off and an allowance of £1,116 is required against the remaining receivables.

You are required to:

(a) Draw up an initial trial balance and set up any suspense account required

(b) Prepare journal entries to clear the suspense account and make all of the year-end adjustments required from the information in the question

(c) Update the ledger accounts for the journal entries

(d) Prepare a statement of profit or loss for the year ending 30 June 20X8 and statement of financial position at that date

6 The following figures have been extracted from a sole trader's trial balance at 31 March 20X5.

	Debit £	Credit £
Inventory at 1 April 20X4	32,000	
Inventory at 31 March 20X5	64,000	64,000
Purchases	250,000	

Complete the table below to show how the sole trader would report these figures if she were to use the cost of goods sold method.

	Debit £	Credit £
Cost of goods sold		
Inventory		

Accounts for partnerships

4

Learning outcomes

5.1	Describe the key components of a partnership agreement
	• What a partnership agreement typically may or may not contain
	• That a formal partnership agreement may not exist for all partnerships
5.2	**Describe the accounting procedures for a change in partners**
	• A simple definition of goodwill in accounting terms
	• Why goodwill will change capital balances on admission or retirement of a partner
	• That goodwill may be introduced and subsequently eliminated from the accounting records using the profit sharing ratio.
	• Calculate the goodwill adjustments using the profit sharing ratio
	• Enter such adjustments in ledger accounts and balance off these accounts as necessary
5.3	**Describe the key components of partnership accounts**
	• The purpose of a statement of profit or loss
	• The purpose and content of the partnership appropriation account
	• How the statement of profit or loss is linked to the partnership appropriation account
	• The nature and content of partners' current accounts
	• The nature and content of partners' capital accounts
	• The purpose of a statement of financial position
5.4	**Prepare a statement of profit or loss for a partnership, in the given format**
	• That the statement of profit or loss for a partnership is an adaptation of one for a sole trader
	• Itemise income and expenditure in line with given organisational policies
	• Transfer data from the trial balance to the appropriate line of the statement according to the level of detail given for the organisation

5.5	Prepare a partnership appropriation account, in compliance with the partnership agreement and in the given format
	• Apply the terms of a partnership agreement
	• Record interest on capital (but not how to calculate it)
	• Record interest on drawings (but not how to calculate it)
	• Record salaries or commission paid to partners
	• Calculate, and appropriate and account for, the residual profit according to the profit sharing ratio
	• Recognise the status of partners' salaries, commission and interest
	• Present this account in the format given for the organisation
5.6	**Prepare the current accounts for each partner**
	• Enter ledger accounting entries
	• Account for drawings in the form of cash, goods or services
	• Link the current account with figures from the appropriation account
5.7	**Prepare a statement of financial position for a partnership, in compliance with the partnership agreement and in the given format**
	• How the statement of financial position for a partnership differs from one of a sole trader
	• Apply the net assets presentation of the statement of financial position
	• Transfer data from the trial balance to the appropriate line of the statement according to the level of detail given for the organisation
	• Show partners' current and capital accounts on the statement of financial position

Assessment context

Partnerships will be tested in Tasks 4 and 5 of the exam. They are likely to test a range of requirements, including calculating the profit available for appropriation; calculating the amount to be appropriated to specific partners; preparing the current and capital accounts; and preparing an appropriation account and/or a statement of financial position. These questions may include changes to the partnership agreement during the period and the admission of a new partner or the retirement of an existing partner (but not both).

Qualification context

Partnerships are examined in *Final Accounts Preparation*.

Business context

Many individuals set up business as a sole trader – as they expand they need new finance. One way of obtaining this is to go into partnership with someone else. That other person could provide some of the finance needed. They may also bring new ideas to the table. Becoming a partnership will mean that the sole trader will share some of their risk, although they will also need to share their profits! It is always recommended that a partnership agreement is drawn up to retain a legal record of how the partnership will operate.

Chapter overview

- Capital and interest on capital
- Drawings and interest on drawings
- Salaries
- Profit sharing ratio (PSR)

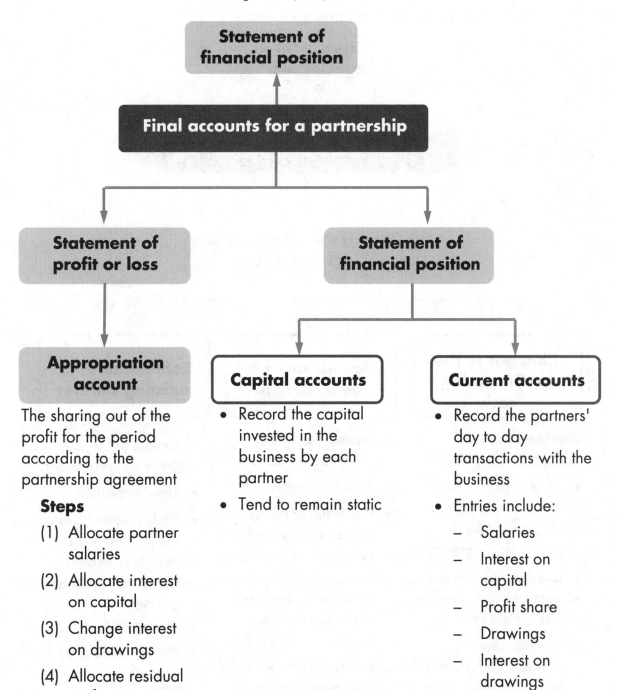

Statement of financial position

Final accounts for a partnership

Statement of profit or loss

Statement of financial position

Appropriation account

The sharing out of the profit for the period according to the partnership agreement

Steps

(1) Allocate partner salaries

(2) Allocate interest on capital

(3) Change interest on drawings

(4) Allocate residual profit using PSR

Capital accounts

- Record the capital invested in the business by each partner
- Tend to remain static

Current accounts

- Record the partners' day to day transactions with the business
- Entries include:
  - Salaries
  - Interest on capital
  - Profit share
  - Drawings
  - Interest on drawings

Chapter overview

To complete a partnership statement of financial position:

- Calculate the current account balances (where required) and include the adjusted balances in the statement of financial position
- Work down the trial balance, transferring the asset, liability and capital balances to the statement of financial position
- Include totals where appropriate

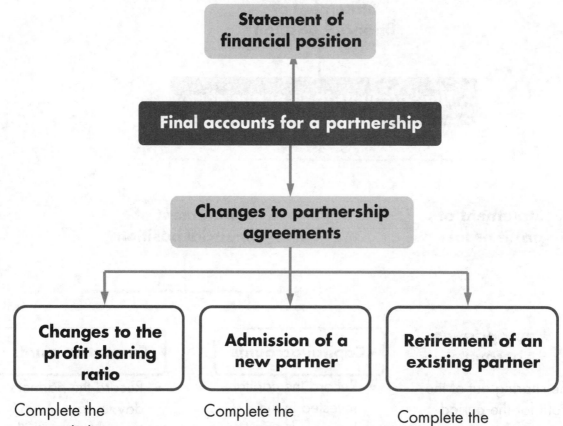

Statement of financial position

Final accounts for a partnership

Changes to partnership agreements

| **Changes to the profit sharing ratio** | **Admission of a new partner** | **Retirement of an existing partner** |

Complete the appropriation account:

- Time apportion to factor in mid-year changes to the partnership agreement
- Use the old partnership agreement for the first plan of the year
- Use the new partnership agreement to appropriate profits for the latter part of the year

Complete the appropriation account:

- Time apportion
- Profits made before the new partner joined will be allocated according to the old partnership agreement, therefore excluding the 'new' partner
- Profits made after the new partner joins will be allocated according to the new agreement

Complete the appropriation account:

- Time apportion
- Profits made before the partner retires will be allocated according to the old partnership agreement
- Profits made after the partner retires will exclude the outgoing partner

Introduction

Definition

> **Partnership –** the relationship which exists between two or more persons carrying on a business with a view to profit

Partnerships are similar to sole traders. With a sole trader, the owner will run the business and any profits belong to him. The sole trader also bears the risk that the business may not be successful.

In a partnership, the owners (partners) run the business together, and share profits and risk.

Most partnerships have **unlimited liability** which means the partners are personally liable for the debts of the business.

Liability is also **joint and several**, so if one partner cannot meet the partnership's obligations, the other partners must make up any shortfall.

Limited liability partnerships (LLPs) exist nowadays to limit partner liability.

Partnership agreements

The partners will need to agree the terms under which the partnership will operate and decide, for example, how much capital each partner will contribute and what share of profits they will be entitled to.

This is done by way of a **partnership agreement** which usually covers the following areas:

Area	Consideration
Capital	• How much each partner pays in • Whether a 'fixed capital' level is specified
Profit sharing ratio (PSR)	• Allocation of profit • More to senior partners? • Equal shares?
Salaries	• Whether or not partners are entitled to salaries • It is an appropriation of profit • It is not an expense in the statement of profit or loss
Interest on capital	• Whether or not allowed • Paid on capital injected • Interest rate
Drawings	• May set a limit • May set an interest charge

A formal partnership agreement is not a requirement for a business relationship to become a partnership. If the partners do not have a formal partnership agreement, then provisions of the Partnership Act 1890 apply.

Accounting for partnerships

There are two key differences between accounting for a sole trader and a partnership. These are illustrated below.

Statement of profit or loss

Sole trader		Partnership	
	£		£
Sales	X	Sales	X
Cost of goods sold	(X)	Cost of goods sold	(X)
Gross profit	X	Gross profit	X
Less expenses	(X)	Less expenses	(X)
Profit for period	X	Profit for period	X

All belongs to sole trader

Shared between partners according to the partnership agreement

The Profit Appropriation Account

The profit for the period is **appropriated** (shared out) between the partners according to their partnership agreement.

Steps

(1)   Allocate the partner salaries

(2)   Allocate any interest on capital

(3)   Charge any interest on drawings

Note. These steps enable us to calculate the profit available for distribution.

Then:

(4)   Allocate remaining profit balance in PSR.

This is done using an **appropriation** account.

Illustration 1: An appropriation account

	£
Net profit	26,000
Salaries:	
Partner A	4,000
Partner B	2,500
Partner C	0
Interest on capital:	
Partner A	500
Partner B	200
Partner C	1,000
Profit available for distribution:	17,800
Profit share:	
Partner A (40%)	7,120
Partner B (20%)	3,560
Partner C (40%)	7,120
Total profit distributed	17,800

This means that the total profit of £26,000 is appropriated between the three partners as follows:

- Partner A   £11,620 (£4,000 + £500 + £7,120)
- Partner B   £6,260 (£2,500 + £200 + £3,560)
- Partner C   £8,120 (£0 + £1,000 + £7,120)

Note. The **profit share** is always the last entry, splitting the residual profit after all other allocations.

Statement of financial position

Sole trader		Partnership	
	£		£
Proprietor's interest		**Capital accounts**	
Capital	X	Partner A	X
Profit	X	Partner B	X
Less drawings	(X)		X
	X	**Current accounts**	
		Partner A	X
		Partner B	X
			X
			X

Amount owed back to the **owner** by the business

Amount owed back to the **partners** by the business

Capital accounts

These represent the capital invested in the business by each individual partner. The balances in these accounts will remain relatively static.

The **capital account** can be shown as one T account subdivided into columns.

For example, if Partner A contributed £5,000 and Partner B £8,000, the capital account would show:

Capital account

	Ptnr A £	Ptnr B £		Ptnr A £	Ptnr B £
			Balance b/d	5,000	8,000

Current accounts

These record each partner's day to day transactions with the business.

The main entries in the **current account** will be the partners' appropriation of profits (salary, interest on capital and profit share) less drawings they have taken from the business and any interest charged on those drawings.

Current account

	Ptnr A £	Ptnr B £		Ptnr A £	Ptnr B £
Drawings	2,900	970	Balance b/d	1,000	1,500
Interest on drawings	100	30	Salaries	1,500	0
			Interest on capital	500	800
Balance c/d	4,000	5,000	Profit share	4,000	3,700
	7,000	6,000		7,000	6,000

Current accounts

These record each partner's day to day transactions with the business.

The main entries in the current account will be the partners' appropriation of profits (salary, interest on capital and profit share) less drawings they have taken from the business and any interest charged on those drawings.

Current account

	Ptnr A £	Ptnr B £		Ptnr A £	Ptnr B £
Drawings	2,900	970	Balance b/d	1,000	1,500
Interest on drawings	100	30	Salaries	1,500	0
			Interest on capital	500	800
Balance c/d	4,000	5,000	Profit share	4,000	3,700
	7,000	6,000		7,000	6,000

The AAT have confirmed the following in relation to questions on partnerships:

General guidance	• The number of partners in a scenario will be **limited to a maximum of three**
	• There will be a **maximum of one change** in the partnership during a period (this means there could be either the admission of a new partner or the retirement of an existing partner, but not both)
	• Where goodwill arises, it will always be introduced and then subsequently eliminated
	• Limited liability partnerships (LLPs) are not examinable
	• The formation of a partnership from a sole trader will not be tested
	• The dissolution of a partnership will not be tested
Specific guidance on the appropriation of profit	• The net profit figure for the period will be given
	• All relevant partnership agreement information will be given
	• A proforma appropriation account will be given
	• Questions may involve a change in profit sharing ratio during the period
	• Interest on capital may need to be calculated accurately according to given information
	• Interest on drawings will not need to be calculated

Having been introduced to partnership accounts, this chapter will now focus more on the practical application of this information and develop the techniques you need to answer questions on this area.

The partnership appropriation account, current accounts and capital accounts

Activity 1: Tick, Cast and Balance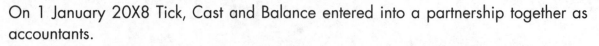

On 1 January 20X8 Tick, Cast and Balance entered into a partnership together as accountants.

The following information is available about the partnership:

• Balance would receive a salary of £15,000 per annum.

• Each partner would receive interest on capital at a rate of 12% per annum.

- Profit share would be as follows:

    - Tick   50%
    - Cast   30%
    - Balance   20%

- They paid in the following capital amounts:

    - Tick   £50,000
    - Cast   £30,000
    - Balance   £20,000

- In the year to 31 December 20X8, their net profit for the period was £50,000.

- During the year, they had made drawings in cash as follows:

    - Tick   £6,000
    - Cast   £4,000
    - Balance   £8,800

When completing the following tasks, where relevant, show clearly the balances carried down.

- You **must** enter zeros where appropriate in order to obtain full marks.
- Do **not** use brackets, minus signs or dashes.

Required

(a) Prepare the capital account for each partner as at 31 December 20X8.

Capital account

	Tick £	Cast £	Balance £		Tick £	Cast £	Balance £

(b) **Prepare the appropriation account for the partnership business for the year ended 31 December 20X8.**

Partnership appropriation account

	£
Profit for appropriation	
Salaries:	
Tick	
Cast	
Balance	
Interest on capital:	
Tick	
Cast	
Balance	
Profit available for distribution	
Profit share:	
Tick	
Cast	
Balance	
Total profit distributed	

(c)   Prepare the current account for each partner as at 31 December 20X8.

Current account

	Tick £	Cast £	Balance £		Tick £	Cast £	Balance £

(d)   Show the partners' capital and current account balances on the statement of financial position.

Tick, Cast and Balance
Statement of financial position as at 31 December 20X8

	£	£	£	£
Net assets				
Financed by	Tick	Cast	Balance	Total

Current accounts

Generally, the partners' current accounts will have a **credit balance** on them.

This indicates that the profits appropriated to the partners are more than the drawings taken by them and any interest on the drawings.

However, it is possible that the current account could have a **debit balance**.

For example, this would arise if the level of profits appropriated is very low or the level of drawings taken is very high.

Effectively it would mean that the particular partner 'owes' money back to the partnership.

This would still be shown in the financing section of the statement of financial position. However, it will be a deduction to the amount partners have contributed to the business.

Illustration 2: Partner accounts

Using a partner called Jeff to illustrate this:

Jeff's partnership accounts:

Account	£
Capital account	20,000 credit
Current account	1,400 debit

Statement of financial position

	£	£	£	£
Net assets				124,230
Financed by	Jeff	Bill	Sid	Total
Capital accounts	**20,000**	40,000	40,000	100,000
Current accounts	**1,400**	14,850	10,780	24,230
	18,600	54,850	50,780	124,230

Salaries, interest on capital and interest on drawings

In Activity 1 *Tick, Cast and Balance* we saw that the terms of the profit share can vary. For example, the terms of the arrangement may be that the partners are:

- Allowed a salary
- Allowed interest on the capital balance that they have within the partnership

Also, partners may be:

- Charged interest on drawings they make

Where relevant, all of these items must be added/deducted to **profit for the year** so that the **profit available for distribution** can be calculated.

The next two examples provide exam-standard practice at partnership tasks.

Activity 2: Cedric, Harry, and Ron

This task is about accounting for partnerships. You have the following information:

- The financial year ends on 31 August.

- The partners are Cedric, Harry, and Ron.

- Interest on capital is allowed at 3.0% per annum on the capital account balances at the end of the financial year.

- Interest on drawings is charged to the partners and is shown in the table below.

Summary of the partnership agreement:

	Cedric £	Harry £	Ron £
Annual salaries	0	16,000	25,000
Capital account balances, 31 August 20X8	60,000	72,000	40,000
Capital account balances, 31 August 20X9	60,000	75,000	44,000
Drawings for the year	24,000	46,000	44,000
Interest on drawings for the year	450	760	800

- The profit for distribution to the partners after appropriations is £90,000.
- Profits are shared in the ratio 4:3:3 with Cedric taking the largest share.

Required

Prepare the current accounts for the partners for the year ended 31 August 20X9. Show clearly the balances carried down.

- **You MUST enter zeros where appropriate in order to obtain full marks.**

- **Do NOT use brackets, minus signs or dashes.**

Solution

Current accounts

	Cedric £	Harry £	Ron £		Cedric £	Harry £	Ron £
Balance b/d		500		Balance b/d	4,000		3,600

Picklist: Balance b/d, Balance c/d, Bank, Capital – Cedric, Capital – Harry, Capital – Ron, Current – Cedric, Current – Harry, Current – Ron, Drawings, Goodwill, Interest on capital, Interest on drawings, Salaries, Share of loss, Share of profit

Activity 3: Anne, George and Timmy

This task is about accounting for partnerships.

You have the following information about a partnership business for the year ended 31 August 20X9:

- The partners are Anne, George and Timmy.

- Interest on capital is allowed at 6% per annum on the opening capital balances. Total interest on capital for the year is £18,720.

- Interest on drawings is charged and is shown in the table below.

- The profit of the partnership for the year before appropriations is £182,000.

	Anne	George	Timmy
Profit share	45%	35%	20%
Interest on drawings	1,800	1,000	–
Annual salaries	22,000	12,000	–
Capital account balances as at 1 September 20X8	150,000	90,000	72,000
Capital account balances as at 1 September 20X9	160,000	100,000	75,000

You are asked to calculate the profit available for distribution for the partnership for the year ended 31 August 20X9.

Required

(a) Calculate the total interest on drawings for the year.

£

(b) Calculate the total salaries for the year.

£

(c) Calculate the profit available for distribution to the partners.

IMPORTANT: Show additions to the profit for the year as positive and deductions as negative.

Partnership:	£
Profit for the year	
Interest on capital	
Interest on drawings	
Salaries	
Profit available for distribution for the year	

You have now been asked to calculate the amount appropriated to Anne for the year.

(d) Calculate Anne's total interest on capital for the year.

£

(e) Calculate the total amount appropriated to Anne for the year.

IMPORTANT: Show amounts due to her as positive and charged to her as negative.

Anne:	£
Interest on capital	
Interest on drawings	
Salary	
Share of profit for distribution	
Total appropriation for the year	

Changes to the partnership agreement

Profits are always appropriated according to the partnership agreement. Therefore, if the terms of the agreement change during the period, this will affect the profit appropriation.

Always use the old partnership agreement to appropriate the profits for the first part of the year; and the new partnership agreement, for the latter part of the year.

Assume profits accrue evenly, unless the question specifies otherwise.

Activity 4: Melanie, Sarah and Angela

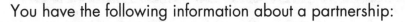

You have the following information about a partnership:

- The financial year ends on 31 December.

- The partners are Melanie, Sarah and Angela.

- The partnership agreement was changed on 1 July 20X9.

- Summary of the partnership agreements:

	Partnership agreement effective until 30 June 20X9			Partnership agreement effective from 1 July 20X9		
	Melanie	Sarah	Angela	Melanie	Sarah	Angela
Profit share	60%	20%	20%	50%	30%	20%
Salary entitlement per annum	nil	£40,000	£20,000	nil	nil	nil

- Profit for the year ended 31 December 20X9 was £400,000 before appropriations, with £180,000 of this being earned in the period from 1 January to 30 June, and £220,000 earned in the period from 1 July to 31 December.

Required

You need to prepare the appropriation account for the partnership business for the year ended 31 December 20X9.

- **You MUST enter zeros where appropriate in order to obtain full marks.**

- **Do NOT use brackets, minus signs or dashes.**

Solution

Partnership appropriation account for the year ended 31 December 20X9

	1 January X9 – 30 June X9 £	1 July X9 – 31 December X9 £	Total £
Profit for appropriation			
Salaries:			
Melanie			
Sarah			
Angela			
Profit available for distribution			

Profit share:			
Melanie			
Sarah			
Angela			
Total profit distributed			

Changes to the partnership – admission of a new partner

Often, when a partnership needs to raise new finance, it will admit a new partner. This individual will bring both finance and (hopefully) experience to the partnership.

The new partner will pay capital into the partnership and this will be credited to their capital account.

All of the partners will then need to agree on a **new partnership agreement** which, as before, will determine the level of salaries, interest on capital and drawings and the PSR. **This new partnership agreement will apply to the period after the new partner has joined.**

Profits made before the new partner joined will be appropriated using the old or existing partnership agreement.

Activity 5: Sam, Grace and Connor

You have the following information about a partnership:

- The financial year ends on 31 July 20X9.

- The partners at the beginning of the year were Sam and Grace and they each had a balance of £10,000 on their current account.

- Connor was admitted to the partnership on 1 November 20X8, when the partnership agreement was changed. Connor introduced capital of £25,000 to the bank account.

	Partnership agreement effective until 31 October 20X8		Partnership agreement effective from 1 November 20X8		
	Sam	Grace	Sam	Grace	Connor
Profit share	60%	40%	30%	50%	20%
Salary entitlement per annum	£12,000	£15,000	£18,000	nil	£13,500

- Under both agreements, partners are allowed interest on capital. This has been calculated as follows:

  - Sam   £1,400 for the 12 months ended 31 July 20X9
  - Grace   £1,200 for the 12 months ended 31 July 20X9
  - Connor   £475 for the 9 months ended 31 July 20X9

You may assume interest for Sam and Grace accrued evenly across the year.

- During the year they had made drawings in cash as follows:

  - Sam   £5,000
  - Grace   £7,000
  - Connor   £3,000

- Profit for the year ended 31 July 20X9 was £120,000 before appropriations. 70% of the profit was earned in the period after Connor joined the partnership.

Required

(a) You need to prepare the appropriation account for the partnership business for the year ended 31 July 20X9.

- **You MUST enter zeros where appropriate in order to obtain full marks.**

- **Do NOT use brackets, minus signs or dashes.**

(b) Prepare the current account for each partner.

Solution

(a) Partnership appropriation account for the year ended 31 July 20X9

	1 Aug 20X8 – 31 Oct 20X8 £	1 Nov 20X8 – 31 July 20X9 £	Total £
Profit for appropriation			
Salaries:			
Sam			
Grace			
Connor			
Interest on capital:			
Sam			
Grace			
Connor			
Profit available for distribution			

Profit share:			
Sam			
Grace			
Connor			
Total profit distributed			

(b) Current accounts

	Sam £	Grace £	Connor £		Sam £	Grace £	Connor £

Picklist: Balance b/d, balance c/d, Bank, Capital – Connor, Capital – Grace, Capital – Sam, Current – Connor, Current – Grace, Current – Sam, Drawings, Goodwill, Interest on capital, Interest on drawings, Salaries, Share of loss, Share of profit

Changes to the partnership – retirement of an existing partner

When a partner retires, they will be allocated their share of the profits which have accrued up to the date of retirement.

Once the profit has been appropriated, the retiring partner's current account needs to be updated.

The final balance on the current account will then be **transferred to the retiring partner's capital account** and this balance will represent the amount they are owed by the partnership.

The balance owed to the retiring partner will then be either paid to them in cash or, if the partnership doesn't have sufficient funds, turned into a loan to the partnership.

The remaining partners will then need to agree on a **new partnership agreement** which, as before, will determine the level of salaries, interest on capital and drawings and the PSR. **This new partnership agreement will apply to the period after the existing partner has retired.**

Activity 6: Jennifer, James and Jonathan (part one)

You have the following information about a partnership:

- The financial year ends on 31 December 20X8.
- The partners at the beginning of the year are Jennifer, James and Jonathan.
- Jennifer retired from the partnership on 30 June 20X8.
- The balance in her capital account at that date was £60,000.

Required

Show the journal entries that would be made if Jennifer were paid off in cash.

Solution

Journal entry

Account name	Debit £	Credit £

In the above example, the partnership had sufficient funds in order to be able to pay Jennifer the balance on her capital account in cash.

This may not always be possible, in which case the partner will lend the partnership the balance on their capital account until it can be repaid.

The balance on the capital account therefore becomes a non-current liability in the statement of financial position and interest may be charged on this loan.

The interest is an expense in the statement of profit or loss and will reduce the net profit which is shared out among the partners in the appropriation account.

Activity 7: Jennifer, James and Jonathan (part two)

Using the information in *Jennifer, James and Jonathan (part one)*, assume Jennifer cannot now be paid the balance on her capital account in cash and so has agreed to lend this amount to the partnership in the form of a long-term loan.

- The financial year ends on 31 December 20X8.

- The partners at the beginning of the year are Jennifer, James and Jonathan.

- Jennifer retired from the partnership on 30 June 20X8.

- The balance in her capital account at that date was £60,000.

- Interest will be paid on the loan at a rate of 10% per annum; interest due is paid on 31 December each year.

- The net profit for the year to 31 December 20X8, before any loan interest, was £80,000.

Required

(a) Show the journal entries that would be made if Jennifer agreed her capital could be treated as a non-current liability by the partnership.

(b) Calculate the revised profit available for distribution, after the loan interest has been deducted.

(c) Prepare an extract to the statement of profit or loss and statement of financial position to reflect the interest on the loan.

Solution

(a) Journal entry

Account name	Debit £	Credit £

(b) Revised profit available for distribution

Working	£

(c) Statement of profit or loss extract for the year ended 31 December 20X8

	£
Expenses	

Statement of financial position extract as at 31 December 20X8

	£
Non-current liabilities	

Changes to the partnership – goodwill

Tangible non-current assets are those assets which are held for long term use and which have a physical form, for example machinery, motor vehicles, computers, etc. Intangible non-current assets are also held for long term use within the business, but they have no physical form. The most common form of intangible non-current asset is goodwill: the extra value in a business that is created by such things as good quality products, excellent after sales service, good location, loyal workforce etc.

When a partner retires from the partnership or a new partner is admitted to the partnership, it is usual for the partners to value the business.

It is likely that the book value of the business (ie the net assets in the statement of financial business) will differ from the price someone would be willing to pay for the business.

The difference may, in part, be due to the increase in value of non-current assets. For example, land and buildings may have increased over their carrying amount.

Also, the difference may be as a result of goodwill. The business may have built up a good reputation and a loyal customer base and the business itself will be worth more than its individual assets.

Therefore, the worth of a business over and above its individual net assets is called **goodwill**.

Illustration 3: Changes to the partnership

A partnership's statement of financial position may have the following assets and liabilities:

	£
Property	200,000
Other assets	120,000
	320,000
Liabilities	(100,000)
	220,000

The business therefore has a **'book value'** of £220,000.

However, when the partnership was valued as a whole, it was judged to be worth £350,000. Therefore, there is a difference of £130,000 above book value.

- £80,000 of this difference was believed to be attributable to the increase in the value of the property.

- The other £50,000 was due to the business's superb regional reputation and wealthy customer base.

- This £50,000 is known as goodwill.

When a partner retires, it is important that they are paid a sum that represents not just the money they invested, but also their share of the extra value created in the business, ie their share of goodwill.

Similarly, when a new partner joins, he will pay in a sum of money (capital). It is important that the original partners value the partnership so they know its worth and can determine how much the partner should contribute.

Goodwill is added to the partners' **capital** accounts according to the existing or **old PSR**.

Account name	Debit £	Credit £
Goodwill	X	
Capital account (using existing PSR)		X

(**Note.** Goodwill is an 'asset' and therefore sits on the debit side of the main ledger.)

Goodwill is an extremely subjective figure and so it is **not** left in the partnership's statement of financial position, but is removed.

This is done using the **new PSR**.

Account name	Debit £	Credit £
Capital accounts (using new PSR)	X	
Goodwill		X

Activity 8: Alan, Karen and Nick

This task is about accounting for partnerships.

You have the following information about a partnership:

- The partners are Alan and Karen.

- Nick was admitted to the partnership on 1 September 20X9 when he introduced £66,000 to the partnership bank account.

- Profit share, effective until 31 August 20X9:

  – Alan   35%
  – Karen   65%

- Profit share, effective from 1 September 20X9:

  – Alan   25%
  – Karen   45%
  – Nick   30%

- Goodwill is valued at £90,000 on 31 August 20X9.

- Goodwill is to be introduced into the accounting records on 31 August and then eliminated on 1 September.

Required

(a) Prepare the capital account for Nick, the new partner, showing clearly the balance carried down on 1 September 20X9.

Capital account – Nick

	£		£
		Balance b/d	0

Picklist: Balance b/d, Balance c/d, Bank, Capital account – Alan, Capital account – Karen, Capital account – Nick, Current account – Alan, Current account – Karen, Current account – Nick, Drawings, Goodwill

Alan is planning to leave the partnership in four years' time. It is estimated Nick's good reputation will have added £20,000 extra value to the goodwill by then.

(b) What will be the amount of goodwill introduced into his capital account at the time of his departure?

£	

This will be		to the goodwill account.

Picklist: a credit, a debit, no change

(c) Why should the rate at which interest is allowed on capital be included in a partnership agreement? Choose ONE answer.

	✓
So that the partners know the amount of profit available for distribution each year	
So that drawings can be calculated	
It provides certainty over the value of the partnership	
So that partners know the rate of return that they will earn on their capital	

Activity 9: Amy and Ben

This task is about accounting for partnerships.

You have the following information about a partnership:

Amy and Ben have been the owners of a partnership business for many years, sharing profits and losses in the ratio 7:3, with Amy receiving the larger share.

On 1 September 20X8, the partnership agreement was changed so that Amy and Ben will share profits and losses in the ratio 6:4, with Amy receiving the larger share.

Goodwill was valued at £110,000 at this date and has already been introduced into the partnership accounting records. It now needs to be eliminated.

Required

(a) **Show the entries required to eliminate the goodwill from the partnership accounting records on 1 September 20X8.**

Account name	Amount £	Debit ✓	Credit ✓

Picklist: Capital – Amy, Capital – Ben, Goodwill

(b) **Complete the following statement regarding Amy's position in the partnership at the end of the day on 1 September 20X8.**

Amy's share of the profits and losses in the partnership has	
after the change in the partnership agreement.	

Picklist: increased, decreased, stayed the same

(c) **Complete the following sentence by selecting the appropriate phrase in each case:**

When a partner retires from a partnership business, the balance on the		
	must be transferred to the	

Picklist: business bank account, partner's capital account, partner's current account

Statement of financial position

We saw earlier that the statement of financial position of a partnership shows that the business is financed by both the partners' capital and current accounts:

Sole trader		Partnership	
	£		£
Proprietor's interest		**Capital accounts**	
Capital	X	Partner A	X
Profit	X	Partner B	<u>X</u>
Less drawings	<u>(X)</u>		X
	<u><u>X</u></u>	**Current accounts**	
		Partner A	X
		Partner B	<u>X</u>
			<u>X</u>
			<u><u>X</u></u>

Amount owed back to the **owner** by the business

Amount owed back to the **partners** by the business

Other than this section, the other parts of the statement of financial position are exactly the same as for the sole trader.

In the exam, you may firstly be asked to make an adjustment (eg calculating the balance on the partners' current accounts). Then the requirement could be to prepare a statement of financial position from a trial balance. A proforma will be provided.

Activity 10: Fred and George

This task is about preparing a partnership statement of financial position.

You are preparing the statement of financial position for the Stone partnership for the year ended 31 August 20X9.

The partners are Fred and George.

You have the final trial balance below. All the necessary year-end adjustments have been made, except for the transfer of a £52,000 profit to the current accounts of the partners. Partners share profits and losses in the ratio 30:70, with George taking the larger share.

Required

(a) **Calculate the balance of each partner's current account after sharing the profits.**

   Indicate whether these balances are DEBIT or CREDIT (the answer fields are not case sensitive).

		Balance	Debit/Credit
Current account: Fred	£		
Current account: George	£		

(b) **Prepare a statement of financial position for the partnership as at 31 August 20X9.**

   You need to use the partners' current account balances that you have just calculated in (a).

   Do not use brackets, minus signs or dashes.

   Picklist: Accruals, Bank, Capital accounts, Cash, Current accounts, Depreciation charges, Expenses, Furniture and fittings, Inventory, Irrecoverable debts, Prepayments, Purchases, Sales, Trade payables, Trade receivables, VAT

Stone partnership

Trial balance as at 31 August 20X9

	Debit £	Credit £
Accruals		5,000
Administration expenses	20,621	
Bank		4,051
Capital account – Fred		25,000
Capital account – George		28,000
Cash	2,600	
Closing inventory	30,980	30,980
Current account – Fred		1,000
Current account – George	800	
Depreciation charges	6,000	
Discounts allowed	1,860	
Furniture and fittings at cost	82,000	
Furniture and fittings accumulated depreciation		10,000
Interest paid	420	
Irrecoverable debts	950	
Opening inventory	27,600	
Prepayments	2,300	
Purchases	200,030	
Purchases ledger control account		24,400
Rent	19,600	
Sales		373,121
Sales ledger control account	36,010	
Travel expenses	14,620	
VAT		5,239
Wages	60,400	
Total	506,791	506,791

Stone partnership

Statement of financial position as at 31 August 20X9

	Cost £	Accumulated depreciation £	Carrying amount £
Non-current assets			
Current assets			
Total current assets			
Current liabilities			
Total current liabilities			
Net current assets			
Net assets			
Financed by:	Fred	George	Total

Alternative presentation of cost of goods sold and inventory

As was discussed in Chapter 3 you may see cost of goods sold and inventory shown on two lines in the trial balance.

This means that the statement of profit or loss balances (opening inventory, purchases, carriage inwards and closing of inventory) have been totalled and shown on the cost of goods sold line.

There is a separate line for closing inventory. This is the asset which will be listed in the statement of financial position at the year end.

This question provides an opportunity to practise completing a statement of financial position under this presentation.

Activity 11: James and Mike

This task is about preparing a partnership statement of financial position.

You are preparing the statement of financial position for the Green Trade partnership for the year ended 31 May 20Y1. The partners are James and Mike.

You have the final trial balance below. All the necessary year-end adjustments have been made, except for the transfer of a £20,000 profit to the current accounts of the partners. Partners share profits and losses in the ratio 1:1.

Required

(a) Calculate the balance of each partner's current account after sharing the profits.

Indicate whether these balances are DEBIT or CREDIT (the answer fields are not case sensitive).

		Balance	Debit/Credit
Current account: James	£		
Current account: Mike	£		

Picklist: Debit, Credit

(b) Prepare a statement of financial position for the partnership as at 31 May 20Y1.

You need to use the partners' current account balances that you have just calculated in (a).

Do not use brackets, minus signs or dashes.

Picklist: Accruals, Bank, Capital accounts, Cash, Current accounts, Inventory, Motor vehicles, Trade payables, Trade receivables, VAT

Green Trade partnership

Trial balance as at 31 May 20Y1

	Debit £	Credit £
Accruals		955
Administration expenses	22,552	
Bank	5,356	
Capital – James		20,000
Capital – Mike		30,000
Cash	242	
Closing inventory	52,352	
Cost of goods sold	122,593	
Current account – James		400
Current account – Mike		650
Depreciation charge	6,353	
Disposal of fixed asset	424	
Motor vehicles at cost	66,324	
Motor vehicles accumulated depreciation		14,643
Allowance for doubtful debts		535
Change in allowance for doubtful debts	52	
Purchases ledger control account		85,130
Sales		205,452
Sales ledger control account	52,564	
Selling expenses	33,478	
VAT		4,525
Total	362,290	362,290

Solution

Green Trade partnership

Statement of financial position as at 31 May 20Y1

	Cost £	Accumulated depreciation £	Carrying amount £
Non-current assets			
Current assets			
Total current assets			
Current liabilities			
Total current liabilities			
Net current assets			
Net assets			
Financed by:	**James**	**Mike**	**Total**

Chapter summary

- A partnership is a number of people in business together trying to make a profit – most partnerships will have a partnership agreement covering the sharing of profits and other financial details.

- Most of the accounting for a partnership is the same as that for a sole trader – the difference lies in accounting for the financing of the partnership in the form of capital, profits and drawings.

- The partners' capital accounts are used to record the permanent capital that a partner pays into the partnership.

- The partners' current accounts are used to record each partner's share of the profits for the year and each partner's drawings during the year.

- The profit appropriation account is used to split the profit for the period between the parties. Profit can be appropriated by salary, interest on capital and interest on drawings, then the remaining profit is appropriated in the profit sharing ratio.

- The financial statements are prepared from the final trial balance – journal entries are required to write up the current accounts with profit share and drawings.

- If a new partner is admitted to the partnership, he or she will pay cash for their share of the partnership assets.

- Goodwill must be adjusted for when the new partner is admitted by crediting the partners' capital accounts in the old profit sharing ratio and debiting the capital accounts in the new profit sharing ratio.

- If a partner retires, goodwill must be adjusted by crediting the partners' capital accounts in the old profit sharing ratio and debiting with the new profit sharing ratio. The retiring partner's current account balance is also transferred to the capital account. The partnership pays the retiring partner what is due, either wholly or partly in cash. Any balance for what is owed remains as a loan from the retiring partner to the partnership.

- If the partners change the profit share ratio during the accounting period, then the appropriation of profit takes place in two separate calculations. The profit for the period is split into the profit before the change, which is appropriated using the old profit sharing ratio, and the profit after the change, which is appropriated using the new profit sharing ratio. Goodwill may also be reallocated at this point.

Keywords

- **Partnership agreement:** agreement between the partners concerning the sharing out of the profits of the partnership and other financial details

- **Profit share:** how the profits of the business are shared among the partners, normally in a ratio such as 2:1

- **Capital accounts:** the accounts that record the permanent capital that each partner pays into the business

- **Current accounts:** the accounts that record the partners' profit share for the year and the partners' drawings for the year

- **Appropriation:** sharing of profit between partners

- **Profit appropriation account:** ledger account used to distribute the profit according to the partnership agreement

- **Tangible non-current assets:** assets held for long-term use in the business which have a physical form eg machinery

- **Intangible non-current assets:** assets held for long-term use in the business which do not have a physical form eg goodwill

- **Goodwill:** an intangible non-current asset which reflects aspects of the business that add value to the business but which are difficult to value eg well-trained workforce, good customer service

Activity answers

Activity 1: Tick, Cast and Balance

(a)

Capital account

	Tick £	Cast £	Balance £		Tick £	Cast £	Balance £
				Bank	50,000	30,000	20,000
Balance c/d	50,000	30,000	20,000				
	50,000	30,000	20,000		50,000	30,000	20,000
				Balance b/d	50,000	30,000	20,000

(b)

Partnership appropriation account

	£
Profit for appropriation	50,000
Salaries:	
Tick	0
Cast	0
Balance	15,000
Interest on capital:	
Tick	6,000
Cast	3,600
Balance	2,400
Profit available for distribution	23,000
Profit share:	
Tick (50%)	11,500
Cast (30%)	6,900
Balance (20%)	4,600
Total profit distributed	23,000

(c)

Current account

	Tick £	Cast £	Balance £		Tick £	Cast £	Balance £
				Salaries	0	0	15,000
Drawings	6,000	4,000	8,800	Interest on capital	6,000	3,600	2,400
				Profit share	11,500	6,900	4,600
Balance c/d	11,500	6,500	13,200				
	17,500	10,500	22,000		17,500	10,500	22,000
				Balance b/d	11,500	6,500	13,200

(d)

Tick, Cast and Balance
Statement of financial position as at 31 December 20X8

	£	£	£	£
Net assets				131,200
Financed by	Tick	Cast	Balance	Total
Capital accounts	50,000	30,000	20,000	100,000
Current accounts	11,500	6,500	13,200	31,200
	61,500	36,500	33,200	131,200

Activity 2: Cedric, Harry and Ron

Current accounts

	Cedric £	Harry £	Ron £		Cedric £	Harry £	Ron £
Balance b/d		500		Balance b/d	4,000		3,600
Drawings	24,000	46,000	44,000	Salaries	0	16,000	25,000
Interest on drawings	450	760	800	Interest on capital	1,800	2,250	1,320
Balance c/d	17,350	0	12,120	Share of profit	36,000	27,000	27,000
				Balance c/d	0	2,010	0
	41,800	47,260	56,920		41,800	47,260	56,920

Activity 3: Anne, George and Timmy

(a) Calculate the total interest on drawings for the year.

£	2,800

(b) Calculate the total salaries for the year.

£	34,000

(c)

Partnership:	£
Profit for the year	182,000
Interest on capital	–18,720
Interest on drawings	2,800
Salaries	–34,000
Profit available for distribution for the year	132,080

(d)

£	9,000

(e)

Anne:	£
Interest on capital	9,000
Interest on drawings	−1,800
Salary	22,000
Share of profit for distribution	59,436
Total appropriation for the year	88,636

Activity 4: Melanie, Sarah and Angela

Partnership appropriation account for the year ended 31 December 20X9

	1 January X9 – 30 June X9 £	1 July X9 – 31 December X9 £	Total £
Profit for appropriation	180,000	220,000	400,000
Salaries:			
Melanie	0	0	0
Sarah	20,000	0	20,000
Angela	10,000	0	10,000
Profit available for distribution	150,000	220,000	370,000

Profit share:			
Melanie (60%/50%)	90,000	110,000	200,000
Sarah (20%/30%)	30,000	66,000	96,000
Angela (20%/20%)	30,000	44,000	74,000
Total profit distributed	150,000	220,000	370,000

Activity 5: Sam, Grace and Connor

(a)

Partnership appropriation account for the year ended 31 July 20X9

	1 Aug 20X8 – 31 Oct 20X8 £	1 Nov 20X8 – 31 July 20X9 £	Total £
Profit for appropriation	36,000	84,000	120,000
Salaries:			
Sam	3,000	13,500	16,500
Grace	3,750	0	3,750
Connor	0	10,125	10,125
Interest on capital:			
Sam	350	1,050	1,400
Grace	300	900	1,200
Connor	0	475	475
Profit available for distribution	28,600	57,950	86,550

Profit share:			
Sam (60%/30%)	17,160	17,385	34,545
Grace (40%/50%)	11,440	28,975	40,415
Connor (0%/20%)	0	11,590	11,590
Total profit distributed	28,600	57,950	86,550

(b)

Current accounts

	Sam £	Grace £	Connor £		Sam £	Grace £	Connor £
				Balance b/d	10,000	10,000	0
Drawings	5,000	7,000	3,000	Salaries	16,500	3,750	10,125
				Interest on capital	1,400	1,200	475
Balance c/d	57,445	48,365	19,190	Share of profit	34,545	40,415	11,590
	62,445	55,365	22,190		62,445	55,365	22,190
				Balance b/d	57,445	48,365	19,190

Activity 6: Jennifer, James and Jonathan (part one)

Journal entry

Account name	Debit £	Credit £
Capital account	60,000	
Bank		60,000

Activity 7: Jennifer, James and Jonathan (part two)

(a)

Journal entry

Account name	Debit £	Credit £
Capital account	60,000	
Loan		60,000

(b)

Revised profit available for distribution

Working	£
Net profit per scenario	80,000
Interest charges	(3,000)
Revised net profit available for distribution	77,000

Tutorial working

Interest charges: £60,000 × 10% × 6/12 = £3,000

(c)

Statement of profit or loss extract for the year ended 31 December 20X8

	£
Expenses	
Interest charges	3,000

Statement of financial position extract as at 31 December 20X8

	£
Non-current liabilities	
Loan	60,000

Activity 8: Alan, Karen and Nick

(a)

Capital account – Nick

	£		£
Goodwill	27,000	Balance b/d	0
Balance c/d	39,000	Bank	66,000
	66,000		66,000

(b)

£	27,500

This will be	a debit	to the goodwill account.

Working

£90,000 + £20,000 = £110,000; £110,000 × 25% = £27,500

(c)

	✓
So that the partners know the amount of profit available for distribution each year	
So that drawings can be calculated	
It provides certainty over the value of the partnership	
So that partners know the rate of return that they will earn on their capital	✓

Activity 9: Amy and Ben

(a)

Account name	Amount £	Debit ✓	Credit ✓
Goodwill	110,000		✓
Capital – Amy	66,000	✓	
Capital – Ben	44,000	✓	

(b)

Amy's share of the profits and losses in the partnership has	decreased
after the change in the partnership agreement.	

(c)

When a partner retires from a partnership business, the balance on the		
partner's current account	must be transferred to the	partner's capital account

---

Activity 10: Fred and George

(a)

		Balance	Debit/Credit
Current account: Fred	£	16,600	Credit
Current account: George	£	35,600	Credit

(b)

Stone partnership

Statement of financial position as at 31 August 20X9

	Cost	Accumulated depreciation	Carrying amount
	£	£	£
Non-current assets			
Furniture and fittings	82,000	10,000	72,000
Current assets			
Inventory		30,980	
Trade receivables		36,010	
Prepayments		2,300	
Cash		2,600	
Total current assets		71,890	
Current liabilities			
Trade payables	24,400		
VAT	5,239		
Accruals	5,000		
Bank	4,051		
Total current liabilities		38,690	
Net current assets			33,200
Net assets			105,200
Financed by:	**Fred**	**George**	**Total**
Capital accounts	25,000	28,000	53,000
Current accounts	16,600	35,600	52,200
	41,600	63,600	105,200

Activity 11: James and Mike

(a)

		Balance	Debit/Credit
Current account: James	£	10,400	Credit
Current account: Mike	£	10,650	Credit

Each partner is entitled to £10,000 of the profit which has been earned during the year (£20,000 × ½).

Before sharing profits, the balance in James's partners' current account is £400 credit. Therefore, after sharing profit, the balance in James's partners' current account is £10,400 (£400 + £10,000).

Before sharing profits, Mike has a credit balance of £650. Therefore, after sharing profits, the balance in Mike's partners' current account is £10,650.

(b)

Green Trade partnership

Statement of financial position as at 31 May 20Y1

	Cost £	Accumulated depreciation £	Carrying amount £
Non-current assets			
Motor vehicles	66,324	14,643	51,681
Current assets			
Inventory		52,352	
Trade receivables		52,029	
Bank		5,356	
Cash		242	
Total current assets		109,979	
Current liabilities			
Trade payables	85,130		
VAT	4,525		
Accruals	955		
Total current liabilities		90,610	
Net current assets			19,369
Net assets			71,050
Financed by:	**James**	**Mike**	**Total**
Capital accounts	20,000	30,000	50,000
Current accounts	10,400	10,650	21,050
	30,400	40,650	71,050

Test your learning

1 **List SIX areas which are likely to be considered when a partnership is drawing up its partnership agreement.**

    -
    -
    -
    -
    -
    -

2 Fred and George started in partnership on 1 May 20X8. Fred paid in £32,000 of capital; and George, £27,000 of capital. During the year ended 30 April 20X9, the business made a profit of £50,000 which is to be split 6:4 between Fred and George. Fred's drawings during the year were £20,000 and George's were £16,000.

    Write up the capital and current accounts for the two partners for the year and show the balances on these accounts that would appear in the statement of financial position at 30 April 20X9.

Capital account – Fred

Date	Details	£	Date	Details	£

Capital account – George

Date	Details	£	Date	Details	£

Current account – Fred

Date	Details	£	Date	Details	£

Current account – George

Date	Details	£	Date	Details	£

Statement of financial position extract

	£	£

3 Jake and Lyle were in partnership with the following partnership agreement:

- Jake receives a salary of £10,000 per annum and Lyle receives a salary of £20,000 per annum.

- Interest on capital is allowed at 4% per annum.

- Profits are to be shared in the ratio of 3:2.

An extract from the trial balance at 30 September 20X8 shows the following:

		£
Capital accounts at 1/10/X7	Jake	100,000
	Lyle	60,000
Current accounts at 1/10/X7	Jake	5,000
	Lyle	8,000
Drawings	Jake	31,000
	Lyle	34,000

The partnership made a profit for the year of £66,400 in the year ending 30 September 20X8.

Prepare the profit appropriation account and the partners' current accounts, and show the figures that will appear in the statement of financial position for the partners' capital and current accounts.

Profit appropriation account

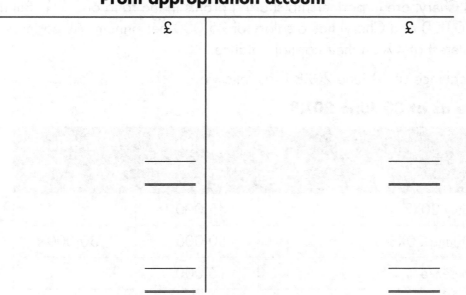

	£		£

Current account – Jake

Date	Details	£	Date	Details	£

Current account – Lyle

Date	Details	£	Date	Details	£

Statement of financial position extract

	£	£

4   Anna, Bill and Cheryl are in partnership sharing profits in the ratio of 2:1:1. Bill has a salary of £10,000 and Cheryl has a salary of £5,000 per annum. All partners are allowed interest at 4% on their capital balance.

The final trial balance at 30 June 20X8 is as follows:

Trial balance as at 30 June 20X8

	Debit £	Credit £
Inventory at 1 July 20X7	45,000	
Inventory at 30 June 20X8	50,000	50,000
Depreciation expense	16,000	
Receivables	50,000	
Irrecoverable debts expense	3,500	
Sales		465,000
Non-current assets at cost	80,000	
Accumulated depreciation at 30 June 20X8		58,000
Allowance for doubtful debts at 30 June 20X8		1,000
Expenses	73,000	
Drawings Anna	38,000	
Bill	15,000	
Cheryl	18,000	
Accruals		5,000
Payables		40,000
Bank	2,000	
Current accounts at 1 July 20X7		
Anna		2,500
Bill		5,000
Cheryl		3,000
Purchases	302,000	
Capital accounts		

	Debit £	Credit £
Anna		30,000
Bill		23,000
Cheryl		10,000
	692,500	692,500

You are required to:

(a) **Prepare the statement of profit or loss for the partnership**
(b) **Complete the profit appropriation account**
(c) **Draw up the partners' current accounts**
(d) **Prepare the statement of financial position as at 30 June 20X8**

5   Kate, Hal and Mary have been in partnership for a number of years sharing profits equally, but on 31 December 20X8 Kate decided to retire. During the year ended 31 December 20X8, the partnership made a profit of £75,000.

The partners' capital and current account balances at 1 January 20X8 and their drawings for the year were as follows:

		£
Capital account	Kate	48,000
	Hal	38,000
	Mary	27,000
Current account	Kate	1,200 (credit)
	Hal	800 (debit)
	Mary	2,500 (credit)
Drawings	Kate	20,000
	Hal	23,500
	Mary	24,400

At 31 December 20X8, the goodwill of the partnership was estimated to be £27,000. After Kate's retirement, profits will be shared equally between the two remaining partners.

It has been agreed that the partnership will pay Kate £15,000 of the amount due to her in cash and that the remainder should remain as a loan to the partnership.

Write up the capital and current accounts for the partners for the year ending 31 December 20X8.

Capital accounts

	Kate £	Hal £	Mary £		Kate £	Hal £	Mary £
	___	___	___		___	___	___
	___	___	___		___	___	___

Current accounts

	Kate £	Hal £	Mary £		Kate £	Hal £	Mary £
	___	___	___		___	___	___
	___	___	___		___	___	___

6 Paul and Gill have been in partnership for a number of years, sharing profits in the ratio of 3:2. On 1 July 20X8, they decided to change the partnership agreement. Gill is to receive a salary of £10,000 per annum and profits are to be distributed in the ratio of 2:1. During the year ending 30 September 20X8, the partnership profits totalled £45,000.

At 1 October 20X7, both partners had credit balances of £2,000 on their current accounts. Paul made drawings of £26,400 during the year to 30 September 20X8 and Gill's drawings for the period totalled £18,700.

Write up the partners' current accounts for the year ending 30 September 20X8.

Current accounts

	Paul £	Gill £		Paul £	Gill £
	___	___		___	___
	___	___		___	___

Introduction to limited company accounts

Learning outcomes

6.1	Describe the main sources of regulation governing company accounts
	• Know the particular importance of maintaining an up-to-date knowledge of relevant legislation and accounting standards that apply to companies
	• Know which source provides the required formats for the statement of profit or loss and statement of financial performance for a company adopting IFRS
	• Know which standards provide guidance for property, plant and equipment, and inventories where IFRS is adopted (recalled as examples of regulation)
6.2	Describe the more detailed reporting arising from these regulations
	• Know the requirement to prepare financial statements at least annually and file them publicly
	• Know why selection and application of accounting policies is regulation, and the objectives that should be met when developing them
	• Know why limited company financial statements need to follow statutory formats, with prescribed headings and terminology
	• Know why cost of sales and other expenses must be classified according to rules
	• Know why taxation is charged in the statement of profit or loss of a company
	• Know why only the carrying value of non-current assets appears on the statement of financial position of a company
	• Know why notes must be provided as part of the financial statements of a company

Assessment context

Questions on this area will be tested in Tasks 4 and 6 of the exam.

Qualification context

The regulatory framework of financial statements is examined throughout your AAT studies.

Business context

The preparation of accounts from different types of organisation is the main source of revenue for a lot of income for smaller accountancy practices. An understanding of the regulatory framework is essential in order to complete the relevant returns in a timely fashion.

Chapter overview

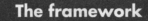

The framework

Accounting standards	*Conceptual framework*	Accounting equation

Accounting standards

- International Accounting Standards (IASs)
- International Financial Reporting Standards (IFRSs)

Conceptual framework

Elements of financial statements

- Assets
- Liabilities
- Equity
- Income
- Expenses

Underlying assumption

- Going concern

Fundamental qualitative characteristics

- Relevance
- Faithful representation

Enhancing qualitative characteristics

- Comparability
- Verifiability
- Timeliness
- Understandability

Accounting equation

- Shows the relationship between the elements of the financial statements
- Assets = Equity + Liabilities

Set of financial statements

- Statement of financial position
- Statement of profit or loss and other comprehensive income
- Statement of changes in equity
- Statement of cash flows
- Notes to the financial statements

Presentation of Financial Statements (IAS 1)

The statement of financial position

Statement of financial position

- Share capital
- Share premium
- Retained earnings
- Revaluation reserve

Principles

- Accruals
- Materiality and aggregation
- Offset
- Comparative information
- Consistency of presentation

Introduction

The regulatory framework

Limited companies are required to observe various rules and regulations when preparing financial statements. These regulations govern the accounting treatment of items and the way in which information is presented.

As we have seen, the purpose of financial statements is to provide useful information about the performance and financial position of an entity. Accounting regulations ensure that financial statements actually do provide useful information.

- Users of the financial statements need to be able to compare the financial statements of different entities and financial statements of the same entity over time. If preparers of financial statements were able to adopt whatever accounting practices they chose it would be impossible to do this in any meaningful way.

- Managers normally wish to show the performance of a company in the best possible light. Without regulation, information might be deliberately presented in such a way as to mislead users.

- The owners or providers of finance to a company are often external to the company and separate from its management. They depend on financial statements for information about a company's performance and position. Accounting regulations ensure that the financial statements provide all the information that users need in order to make decisions.

Sources of regulation

In the UK, the most important sources of regulation for limited companies are:

- Companies legislation (the Companies Act 2006)
- Accounting standards

What are accounting standards?

Accounting standards are authoritative statements of how particular types of transactions and other events should be reflected in financial statements. An entity normally needs to comply with accounting standards in order to produce financial statements which give a fair presentation of its performance and financial position.

It follows that unless there are exceptional circumstances, limited companies must comply with all relevant accounting standards. Sole traders and partnerships often adopt accounting standards, even though they may not be legally obliged to do so.

Although accounting standards state how particular items should be dealt with, many accounting standards set out principles, rather than detailed rules. Preparers of financial statements should be guided by the spirit and reasoning behind accounting standards and not simply regard them as a set of rules to circumvent.

Two sets of accounting standards operate in the UK:

- UK accounting standards issued by the UK Accounting Standards Board (ASB). These are known as Financial Reporting Standards (FRSs) or Statements of Standard Accounting Practice (SSAPs).

- International accounting standards (IASs) or International Financial Reporting Standards (IFRSs) issued by the International Accounting Standards Board (IASB).

Publishing the accounts

At present, unless they are quoted companies, UK companies have a choice when preparing accounts for publication:

- They can follow UK standards. This means that they must follow certain rules set out in the Companies Act itself; these set out the format of the profit and loss account and the balance sheet, the accounting principles to be followed, and other disclosures that must be made.

- They can follow IASs and IFRSs. This means that they comply with IAS 1 *Presentation of Financial Statements*, which contains requirements that are very similar to those in the Companies Act.

Quoted companies must prepare IFRS accounts.

Financial statements for limited companies

IFRS financial statements

Presentation of Financial Statements (IAS 1)

IAS 1 applies to the preparation and presentation of general purpose financial statements in accordance with IFRSs.

This standard emphasises the general objectives of financial statements which are also outlined in the *Conceptual Framework*:

'The objective of general purpose financial reporting is to provide financial information about the reporting entity that is useful to existing and potential investors, lenders and other creditors in making decisions about providing resources to the entity.'

IAS 1 *Presentation of Financial Statements* (para. 36) states that a complete set of financial statements should be prepared at least annually.

A complete set of financial statements comprises:

- A statement of financial position

- A statement of profit or loss and other comprehensive income

- A statement of changes in equity

- A statement of cash flows

- Notes, comprising a summary of significant accounting policies and other explanatory information

In addition, the entity must clearly display:

(a) The name of the company
(b) The date of the financial statements
(c) The currency in which the financial statements are presented
(d) The level of rounding (eg £000 or £ million)

(IAS 1: para. 10)

Comparison with sole traders

The statement of profit or loss provides information about the financial performance of a business. It shows the income generated and the expenditure incurred during an accounting period.

You are familiar with preparing the statement of profit or loss for sole traders and partnerships, and many of the account names you have studied are also relevant when preparing company accounts.

However, certain headings are used when preparing company accounts.

Proforma – statement of profit or loss

XYZ Ltd
Statement of profit or loss for the year ended 31 December 20X2

	20X2 £000	20X1 £000
Revenue	X	X
Cost of sales	(X)	(X)
Gross profit	X	X
Distribution costs	(X)	(X)
Administrative expenses	(X)	(X)
Profit from operations	X	X
Finance costs	(X)	(X)
Profit before tax	X	X
Tax	(X)	(X)
Profit for the year from continuing operations	X	X

Proforma – statement of financial position

A statement of financial position shows the assets, liabilities and equity of a business at a stated date.

XYZ Ltd
Statement of financial position as at 31 December 20X2

	20X2	20X1
	£000	£000
ASSETS		
Non-current assets		
Intangible assets	X	X
Property, plant and equipment	X	X
	X	X
Current assets		
Inventories	X	X
Trade and other receivables	X	X
Cash and cash equivalents	X	X
	X	X
Total assets	X	X
EQUITY AND LIABILITIES		
Equity		
Share capital	X	X
Share premium	X	X
Retained earnings	X	X
Revaluation reserve	X	X
Total equity	X	X
Non-current liabilities		
Bank loans	X	X
	X	X
Current liabilities		
Trade and other payables	X	X
Short-term borrowings	X	X
Tax liability	X	X
	X	X
Total liabilities	X	X
Total equity and liabilities	X	X

While there are many similarities with the accounts for sole traders and partnerships, you'll notice that company financial statements include some additional items, such as:

- Intangible assets
- Share capital
- Share premium
- Retained earnings
- Revaluation reserve
- Bank loans
- Tax

You will encounter these items as you continue your studies.

Further analysis

Items in the statement of financial position should be analysed further when necessary.

The analysis is often shown in notes to the financial statements.

Examples of items which are often analysed are:

- Property, plant and equipment
- Inventories
- Trade and other receivables
- Trade and other payables

Notes to the financial statements

Notes provide or disclose information which is not presented in the statement of profit or loss and other comprehensive income, the statement of financial position, the statement of changes in equity or the statement of cash flows:

- Where it is required by other IFRSs

- Where additional information is relevant to understand any of the financial statements

Typically, many of the notes provide further analysis of the totals shown in the main financial statements. For example, the note to 'trade and other payables' provides an analysis of this balance, and will show amounts arising from trade payables, accruals and other payables.

Accounting policies

Accounting policies are the specific principles, conventions and practices applied by an entity in preparing and presenting the financial statements.

The notes to the financial statements will also disclose the accounting policies adopted by the directors of the financial statements. For example, they will disclose whether property, plant and equipment is held at cost or revaluation.

Property, Plant and Equipment (IAS 16)

IAS 16 sets out the way in which items of property, plant and equipment should be treated in the financial statements.

Property, plant and equipment are tangible items that:

• are held for use in the production or supply of goods or services, for rental to others, or for administrative purposes; and

• are expected to be used during more than one period.

(IAS 16: para. 6)

'Tangible' means that the item has physical substance.

Inventories (IAS 2)

The basic rule per IAS 2 *Inventories* is:

'Inventories should be measured at the **lower of cost and net realisable value**.'(IAS 2: para. 9)

This is an example of **'prudence'** in presenting financial information.

The elements of financial statements

The *Conceptual Framework* defines elements of financial statements. The definitions reduce confusion over which items ought to be recognised and which should not (if an item is not one of the defined elements of financial statements it should not feature in the financial statements).

The five elements of financial statements and their definitions are:

> **Asset**
> A resource **controlled** by an entity as a result of **past events** and from which future **economic benefits** are expected to flow to the entity.

> **Liability**
> A **present obligation** of the entity arising from **past events**, the settlement of which is expected to result in an **outflow** from the entity of resources embodying economic benefits.

> **Equity**
> The residual interest in the assets of an entity after deducting all its liabilities, so
> EQUITY = NET ASSETS = SHARE CAPITAL + RESERVES

> **Income**
> Increase in economic benefits during the accounting period in the form of **inflow** or enhancements **of assets or decrease of liabilities** that result in increases in equity, **other than** those relating to **contributions from equity participants**.

> **Expenses**
> Decrease in economic benefits during the accounting period in the form of **outflows** or depletions **of assets or increases of liabilities** that result in decreases in equity, **other than those relating to distributions to equity participants**.

(IASB, 2010)

The *Conceptual Framework* definitions demonstrate that IFRSs are based on a statement of financial position approach to recognition, ie income and expenses are defined as changes in assets and liabilities, rather than the other way round.

Recognition of the elements of financial statements

Recognition is the process of showing an item in the financial statements, with a description in words and a number value.

An item is recognised in the statement of financial position or the statement of profit or loss and other comprehensive income when:

(a)   It meets the definition of an element of the financial statements; and

(b)   It is probable that any future economic benefit associated with the item will flow to or from the entity; and

(c)   The item has a cost or value that can be measured with reliability.

Hence, recognition relies heavily upon a good assessment of probability of whether economic benefits will flow to or from the entity.   (IASB, 2010)

Accounting equation

The relationship between these elements is shown by the accounting equation:

Assets = Equity + Liabilities

Rearranged: Assets – Liabilities = Equity

Equity = Contributions from owners + Income – Expenses – Distributions to owners

Therefore if net assets increase, it is either as a result of income or from a contribution. In the same way, if net assets decrease, it is either an expense or a distribution.

Activity 1: Elements of the financial statements

A resource controlled by an entity as a result of a past event and from which future economic benefits are expected to flow to the entity.

Required

(a) This statement describes:

an asset	
a liability	
equity	
income	
expenses	

The residual interest in the assets of an entity after deducting all its liabilities.

(b) This statement describes:

an asset	
a liability	
equity	
income	
expenses	

A distribution to equity participants is an expense.

(c) Is this statement true or false?

True	
False	

Measuring the elements of financial statements

Measurement is the process of determining the monetary amounts at which the elements of the financial statements are to be recognised and carried in the statement of financial position and statement of profit or loss and other comprehensive income. There are four key measurement techniques for you to be aware of:

Historical (this is the most commonly used) Measured at the amount paid at transaction date	**Current cost** Measured at the amount that would be paid if the transaction occurred today
Realisable value (settlement value) Measured at the amount that could be obtained if the asset were sold, or liability realised, today	**Present value** Measured at the discounted value of all future cash flows

Activity 2: Measurement bases

A number of different measurement bases are used in the financial statements.

Required

(a) Match the measurement bases with an appropriate example.

A company can sell machine A for £9,000.	
If a company had to buy machine B now, it would pay £20,000.	
Machine C will be used by a company to generate sales. It is expected to generate discounted net cash flows of £20,000 over the next 5 years.	
3 years ago, machine D cost the company £15,000.	

Picklist: Current cost, Historical cost, Present value, Realisable value

An asset was purchased for £20,000. It is estimated that it will generate a net cash inflow of £30,000 for the business, and that it can be sold for £25,000. An identical asset can now be purchased for £22,000.

(b) Measuring the asset under the historical cost basis, the asset will be recorded at:

£20,000	
£22,000	
£25,000	
£30,000	

Chapter summary

- Financial information must be presented fairly if it is to be useful. This normally means that it must comply with all applicable regulations

- Regulations ensures that:

  - Users are able to compare the financial statements of different companies and of the same company over time

  - Users are not deliberately misled by the financial statements

  - Financial statements provide the information that users need

- The most important sources of regulation in the UK are:

  - The Companies Act 2006
  - Accounting Standards

- International Accounting Standards (IASs) and International Financial Reporting Standards (IFRSs) are issued by the International Accounting Standards Board (IASB)

- The Companies Act 2006 states that the directors of a limited company must file annual accounts

- Published IFRS accounts consist of:

  - A statement of financial position
  - A statement of profit or loss and other comprehensive income
  - A statement of changes in equity
  - A statement of cash flows
  - Notes

Keywords

- **Accounting standards:** authoritative statements of how particular types of transactions and other events should be reflected in financial statements

- **Companies Act accounts:** published accounts that comply with the accounting rules in the Companies Act 2006 and with the requirements of UK accounting standards

- **Conceptual framework:** a set of concepts and principles that underpin the preparation of financial statements

- **Current cost:** assets are carried at the amount of cash that would have to be paid if the same or a similar asset was acquired currently

- **Historical cost:** assets are recorded at the amount of cash paid or the fair value of the consideration given to acquire them at the time of the acquisition

- **IFRS accounts:** published accounts that comply with the requirements of IFRS/IAS

- **Present value:** assets are carried at the present discounted value of the future net cash inflows that the item is expected to generate in the normal course of business

- **Published accounts/financial statements:** the financial statements of limited companies that are circulated to shareholders and filed with the Registrar of Companies (also referred to as **statutory accounts**)

- **Realisable value:** assets are carried at the amount of cash that could currently be obtained by selling the asset

Activity answers

Activity 1: Elements of the financial statements

(a)

an asset	✓
a liability	
equity	
income	
expenses	

(b)

an asset	
a liability	
equity	✓
income	
expenses	

(c)

True	
False	✓

Activity 2: Measurement bases

(a)

A company can sell machine A for £9,000.	Realisable value
If a company had to buy machine B now, it would pay £20,000.	Current cost
Machine C will be used by a company to generate sales. It is expected to generate discounted net cash flows of £20,000 over the next 5 years.	Present value
3 years ago, machine D cost the company £15,000.	Historical cost

(b)

£20,000	✓
£22,000	
£25,000	
£30,000	

1   If a limited company becomes insolvent, the maximum amount that the shareholders can lose is the amount that they have invested in the company.

    Is this statement true or false?

True	
False	

2   In the UK, limited companies must observe the requirements of the Companies Act 2006 and of accounting standards when preparing financial statements.

    Explain why accounting regulation is needed.

3   The Companies Act 2006 sets out the duties and responsibilities of limited company directors.

    Which of the following is NOT a legal responsibility of the directors?

To prepare and approve the annual accounts	
To file the accounts with the Registrar of Companies	
To keep accounting records that are neutral, complete and free from error	
To ensure that the accounts show a true and fair view	

4   The IASB's *Conceptual Framework for Financial Reporting* is an accounting standard.

    Is this statement true or false?

True	
False	

5   Stevens Ltd uses an item of plant. The directors have calculated that the total sales revenue from the goods produced over the remaining life of the plant, less the costs of operating it, will be £200,000 after adjusting the amounts to reflect the time value of money.

    This amount of £200,000 is the plant's:

Current cost	
Fair value	
Historical cost	
Present value	

Test your learning: answers

CHAPTER 1   Organisations and their financial accounts

1

	Debit £	Credit £	Type of balance	P/L or SFP
Sales		41,200	Income	P/L
Loan		1,500	Liability	SFP
Wages	7,000		Expense	P/L
Non-current assets	7,100		Asset	SFP
Opening inventory	1,800		Expense	P/L
Receivables	3,400		Asset	SFP
Discounts received		40	Income	P/L
Postage	100		Expense	P/L
Bank	300		Asset	SFP
Capital		9,530	Capital	SFP
Rent	500		Expense	P/L
Purchases	30,100		Expense	P/L
Payables		2,500	Liability	SFP
Discounts allowed	70		Expense	P/L
Drawings	3,000		Reduction of capital	SFP
Electricity	800		Expense	P/L
Telephone	600		Expense	P/L
	54,770	54,770		

2   (a)   The gross profit of a business is the profit from the trading activities.

(b)   The total of the current assets minus the current liabilities is known as net current assets.

(c)   Current liabilities are amounts that are payable within one year.

(d)   Long-term liabilities are amounts payable after more than one year.

3   Materiality concept

4   The four objectives that should be considered when selecting appropriate accounting policies are relevance, reliability, comparability and ease of understanding.

Financial information is relevant if it has the ability to influence the economic decisions of users of that information and is provided in time to influence those decisions. Materiality affects relevance.

Reliable information is a wider concept. In order for information to be reliable, it must represent the substance of the transaction or event, it must be free from bias and material error and, if there is uncertainty about the information, then a degree of caution or prudence must have been applied in making any judgements.

The information in financial statements should be comparable over time and, as far as possible, between different businesses. Therefore, the accounting policies chosen should be applied consistently.

Finally, accounting policies should be chosen to ensure ease of understanding by users of the financial statements. Users can be assumed to have a reasonable knowledge of business and economic activities and accounting and a willingness to study the information diligently.

5

Consistency	
Going concern	
Relevance	✓
Timeliness	

CHAPTER 2 Incomplete records

1   Drawings = £15,300

	£
Opening net assets	58,900
Closing net assets	71,400
Increase in net assets	12,500

Increase in net assets	=	capital introduced + profit – drawings
£12,500	=	£10,000 + 17,800 – drawings
Drawings	=	£15,300

2   Purchases = £59,100

Payables account

	£		£
Payments	56,900	Balance b/d	3,800
Discounts	1,300		
Balance c/d	4,700	Purchases (bal fig)	59,100
	62,900		62,900

3   Drawings = £11,730

Bank account

	£		£
Balance b/d	1,020	Purchases	24,600
Receipts	48,700	Expenses	12,500
		Drawings (bal fig)	11,730
		Balance c/d	890
	49,720		49,720

4   Cost of sales = £127,000

	%	£
Sales	145	184,150
Cost of sales	100	127,000
Gross profit	45	57,150

5   Sales = £200,000

	%	£
Sales	100	200,000
Cost of sales	65	130,000
Gross profit	35	70,000

Receivables account

	£		£
Balance b/d	10,400	Receipts	108,500

Payables account

	£		£
Payments	74,400	Balance b/d	6,200
Balance c/d	8,300	Purchases (bal fig)	76,500
	82,700		82,700

Cost structure:

	%
	%
Sales	140
Cost of sales	100
Gross profit	40

If purchases are £76,500 then the cost of sales is:

	£
Opening inventory	7,600
Purchases	76,500
	84,100
Less closing inventory	(6,100)
	78,000

Using the cost structure the sales figure can be determined:

Cost structure:

	%	£
Sales	140	109,200
Cost of sales	100	78,000
Gross profit	40	31,200

The sales figure can then be entered into the receivables account and the closing balance found.

Receivables account

	£		£
Balance b/d	10,400	Receipts	108,500
Sales	109,200	Balance c/d	11,100
	119,600		119,600

The statement of profit or loss can now be prepared:

Statement of profit or loss for the year ended 31 March 20X9

	£	£
Sales revenue		109,200
Less cost of sales		
Opening inventory	7,600	
Purchases	76,500	
	84,100	
Less closing inventory	(6,100)	
		(78,000)
Gross profit		31,200
Less expenses		
Expenses (12,600 – 800 + 600)	12,400	
Depreciation	1,600	
		(14,000)
Profit for the year		17,200

In order to draw up the statement of financial position, we need the opening capital and the drawings figures.

Net assets at 1 April 20X8

	£
Bank	430
Inventory	7,600
Receivables	10,400
Payables	(6,200)
Accrual	(800)
Non-current assets	12,600
Opening capital	24,030

The drawings can be found as the balancing figure in the bank account:

Bank account

	£		£
Balance b/d	430	Payables	74,400
Receipts from receivables	108,500	Expenses	12,600
		Drawings (bal fig)	14,730
		Balance c/d	7,200
	108,930		108,930

Statement of financial position as at 31 March 20X9

	£	£	£
Non-current assets (12,600 – 1,600)			11,000
Current assets:			
Inventory		6,100	
Receivables		11,100	
Bank		7,200	
		24,400	
Current liabilities:			
Payables	8,300		
Accruals	600		
		(8,900)	
Net current assets			15,500
			26,500
Financed by:			
Opening capital			24,030
Add profit for the year			17,200
			41,230
Less drawings			(14,730)
			26,500

7   Closing inventory = £6,000

Cost structure:

	%	£
Sales	100	240,000
Cost of sales	70	168,000
Gross profit	30	72,000

	£	£
Sales		240,000
Less cost of sales		
Opening inventory	12,000	
Purchases	162,000	
	174,000	
Less closing inventory	?	
		168,000
Gross profit		72,000

Therefore the closing inventory value must be £6,000.

CHAPTER 3   Accounts for sole traders

1   The capital balance at 30 June 20X8 is £33,452.

	£
Opening capital	34,560
Net profit	48,752
	83,312
Less drawings	(49,860)
Closing capital	33,452

2
			£	£
(a)	DEBIT	Drawings	1,500	
	CREDIT	Purchases		1,500
or				
(b)	DEBIT	Drawings	2,100	
	CREDIT	Sales		2,100

3   Telephone expense = £3,400 + £300   = £3,700
    Insurance expense = £1,600 – 200   = £1,400

4   **Depreciation charge:**
    Fixtures and fittings   (12,600 × 20%)   = £2,520
    Motor vehicles   (38,500 – 15,500) × 30% = £6,900
    Accumulated depreciation:
    Furniture and fittings   3,400 + 2,520   = £5,920
    Motor vehicles   15,500 + 6,900   = £22,400

Non-current assets

	Cost	Accumulated depreciation	Carrying amount
	£	£	£
Furniture and fittings	12,600	5,920	6,680
Motor vehicles	38,500	22,400	16,100
			22,780

5   (a)   Initial trial balance

	Debit £	Credit £
Sales		308,000
Machinery at cost	67,400	
Office equipment at cost	5,600	
Office costs	2,300	
Distribution costs	4,100	
Sales ledger control	38,400	
Telephone expenses	1,800	
Purchases ledger control		32,100
Heat and light	3,100	
Bank overdraft		3,600
Purchases	196,000	
Petty cash	100	
Insurance	4,200	
Accumulated depreciation – machinery		31,200
Accumulated depreciation – office equipment		3,300
Inventory at 1 July 20X7	16,500	
Loan from bank		10,000
Miscellaneous expenses	2,200	
Wages	86,700	
Loan interest	600	
Capital		60,000

Initial trial balance

	Debit	Credit
Drawings	20,000	
Allowance for doubtful debts		1,000
Suspense	200	
	44,200	449,200

(b) **Journal entries**

		Debit £	Credit £
(i)	Heat and light	200	
	Suspense		200
(ii)	Inventory – statement of financial position	18,000	
	Inventory – profit or loss		18,000
(iii)	Depreciation expense – machinery		
	((67,400 – 31,200) × 30%)	10,860	
	Accumulated depreciation – machinery		10,860
	Depreciation expense – office equipment		
	(5,600 × 20%)	1,120	
	Accumulated depreciation – office equipment		1,120
(iv)	Loan interest	200	
	Telephone	400	
	Accruals		600
(v)	Prepayments (800 × 3/12)	200	
	Insurance		200
(vi)	Irrecoverable debts expense	1,200	
	Sales ledger control		1,200
	Allowance for doubtful debts adjustment (1,116 – 1,000)	116	
	Allowance for doubtful debts		116

(c) **Ledger accounts**

(i)

Heat and light

		£			£
30 June	Balance b/d	3,100			
30 June	Journal	200	30 June	Balance c/d	3,300
		3,300			3,300
30 June	Balance b/d	3,300			

Suspense account

		£			£
30 June	Balance b/d	200	30 June	Journal	200

(ii)

Inventory – statement of financial position

		£			£
30 June	Journal	18,000			

Inventory – profit or loss

		£			£
			30 June	Journal	18,000

(iii)

Depreciation expense – machinery

		£			£
30 June	Journal	10,860			

Accumulated depreciation – machinery

		£			£
			30 June	Balance b/d	31,200
30 June	Balance c/d	42,060	30 June	Journal	10,860
		42,060			42,060
			30 June	Balance b/d	42,060

Depreciation expense – office equipment

		£			£
30 June	Journal	1,120			

Accumulated depreciation – office equipment

		£			£
			30 June	Balance b/d	3,300
30 June	Balance c/d	4,420	30 June	Journal	1,120
		4,420			4,420
			30 June	Balance b/d	4,420

(iv)

Loan interest

		£			£
30 June	Balance b/d	600			
30 June	Journal	200	30 June	Balance c/d	800
		800			800
30 June	Balance b/d	800			

Telephone

		£			£
30 June	Balance b/d	1,800			
30 June	Journal	400	30 June	Balance c/d	2,200
		2,200			2,200
30 June	Balance b/d	2,200			

Accruals

		£			£
			30 June	Journal	600

(v)

Prepayments

		£			£
30 June	Balance b/d	200			

Insurance

		£			£
30 June	Balance b/d	4,200	30 June	Journal	200
		_____	30 June	Balance c/d	4,000
		4,200			4,200
30 June	Balance b/d	4,000			

(vi)

Irrecoverable debts expense

		£			£
30 June	Journal	1,200			

Sales ledger control

		£			£
30 June	Balance c/d	38,400	30 June	Journal	1,200
		_____	30 June	Balance c/d	37,200
		38,400			38,400
30 June	Balance b/d	37,200			

Allowance for doubtful debts adjustment

		£			£
30 June	Journal	116			

Allowance for doubtful debts

		£			£
			30 June	balance b/d	1,000
30 June	Balance c/d	1,116	30 June	Journal	116
		1,116			1,116
			30 June	Balance b/d	1,116

(d) **Statement of profit or loss for the year ending 30 June 20X8**

	£	£
Sales revenue		308,000
Cost of sales		
Opening inventory	16,500	
Purchases	196,000	
	212,500	
Less closing inventory	(18,000)	
		(194,50)
Gross profit		113,500
Less expenses		
Office costs	2,300	
Distribution costs	4,100	
Telephone	2,200	
Heat and light	3,300	
Insurance	4,000	
Miscellaneous expenses	2,200	
Wages	86,700	
Loan interest	800	
Depreciation – machinery	10,860	
	£	£
Depreciation – office equipment	1,120	
Allowance for doubtful debts adjustment	116	
Irrecoverable debts	1,200	
		118,896
Loss for the year		(5,396)

Statement of financial position as at 30 June 20X8

	Cost £	Accumulated depreciation £	Carrying value £
Non-current assets:			
Machinery	67,400	42,060	25,340
Office equipment	5,600	4,420	1,180
	73,000	46,480	26,520
Current assets:			
Inventory		18,000	
Receivables	37,200		
Less allowance	(1,116)		
		36,084	
Prepayments		200	
Petty cash		100	
		54,384	
Current liabilities:			
Payables	32,100		
Bank overdraft	3,600		
Accruals	600		
		36,300	
Net current assets			18,084
			44,604
Long-term loan			(10,000)
			34,604
Capital			60,000
Loss for the year			(5,396)
			54,604
Less drawings			(20,000)
			34,604

6

	Debit £	Credit £
Cost of goods sold – profit or loss	218,000	
Inventory – statement of financial position	64,000	

Workings:

Inventory at 1 April 20X4	32,000
Purchases	250,000
Inventory at 31 March 20X5	(64,000)
Cost of goods sold	218,000

CHAPTER 4   Accounts for partnerships

1 • How much capital each partner should introduce

   • Whether there should be any restrictions on partners taking drawings out of the business

   • Whether interest on capital should be allowed

   • Whether interest on drawings should be charged

   • Whether partners should be allowed any salaries

   • How the profit should be shared between the partners

2

Capital account – Fred

Date	Details	£	Date	Details	£
			1 May 20X8	Bank	32,000

Capital account – George

Date	Details	£	Date	Details	£
			1 May 20X8	Bank	27,000

Current account – Fred

Date	Details	£	Date	Details	£
30 Apr 20X9	Drawings	20,000	30 Apr 20X9	Profit share	30,000
30 Apr 20X9	Balance c/d	10,000			
		30,000			30,000
			1 May 20X9	Balance b/d	10,000

Current account – George

Date	Details	£	Date	Details	£
30 Apr 20X9	Drawings	16,000	30 Apr 20X9	Profit share	20,000
30 Apr 20X9	Balance c/d	4,000			
		20,000			20,000
			1 May 20X9	Balance b/d	4,000

Statement of financial position extract

	£	£
Capital accounts:		
Fred		32,000
George		27,000
		59,000
Current accounts:		
Fred	10,000	
George	4,000	
		14,000
		73,000

3

Profit appropriation account

	£		£
Salaries			
: Jake	10,000	Profit for the year	66,400
Lyle	20,000		
Interest:			
Jake (100,000 × 4%)	4,000		
Lyle (60,000 × 4%)	2,400		
Balance c/d	30,000		
	66,400		66,400
		Balance b/d	30,000
Profit share:			
Jake (30,000 × 3/5)	18,000		
Lyle (30,000 × 2/5)	12,000		
	30,000		30,000

Current account – Jake

	£		£
Drawings	31,000	Balance b/d	5,000
		Salary	10,000
		Interest	4,000
Balance c/d	6,000	Profit share	18,000
	37,000		37,000
		Balance b/d	6,000

Current account – Lyle

	£		£
Drawings	34,000	Balance b/d	8,000
		Salary	20,000
		Interest	2,400
Balance c/d	8,400	Profit share	12,000
	42,400		42,400
		Balance b/d	8,400

Statement of financial position extract

	£	£
Capital accounts Jake	100,000	
Lyle	60,000	
		160,000
Current accounts Jake	6,000	
Lyle	8,400	
		14,400
		174,400

4 (a) Statement of profit or loss for the year ending 30 June 20X8

	£	£
Sales revenue		465,000
Less: cost of sales		
opening inventory	45,000	
purchases	302,000	
	347,000	
Less closing inventory	(50,000)	
		(297,000)
Gross profit		168,000
Less: expenses	73,000	
depreciation	16,000	
irrecoverable debts	3,500	
		92,500
Profit for the year		75,500

(b) **Profit appropriation account**

		£	£
Profit for the year			75,500
Salaries Bill		10,000	
Cheryl		5,000	
			(15,000)
Interest on capital			
Anna	30,000 × 4%	1,200	
Bill	23,000 × 4%	920	
Cheryl	10,000 × 4%	400	
			(2,520)
Profit available for distribution			57,980
Profit share			
Anna	57,980 × 2/4	28,990	
Bill	57,980 × 1/4	14,495	
Cheryl	10,000 × 4%	14,495	
			57,980

(c) **Current accounts**

Current account – Anna

	£		£
Drawings	38,000	Balance b/d	2,500
		Interest	1,200
		Profit share	28,990
		Balance c/d	5,310
	38,000		38,000
Balance b/d	5,310		

Current account – Bill

	£		£
Drawings	15,000	Balance b/d	5,000
		Salary	10,000
		Interest	920
Balance c/d	15,415	Profit share	14,495
	30,415		30,415
		Balance b/d	15,415

Current account – Cheryl

	£		£
Drawings	18,000	Balance b/d	3,000
		Salary	5,000
		Interest	400
Balance c/d	4,895	Profit share	14,495
	22,895		22,895
		Balance b/d	4,895

(d) **Statement of financial position as at 30 June 20X8**

	Cost £	Accumulated depreciation £	Carrying amount £
Non-current assets	80,000	58,000	22,000
Current assets			
Inventory		50,000	
Receivables	50,000		
Less allowance	(1,000)		
		49,000	
Bank		2,000	
		101,000	

	Cost £	Accumulated depreciation £	Carrying amount £
Current liabilities			
Payables	40,000		
Accrual	5,000		
		(45,000)	
Net current assets			56,000
			78,000
Capital accounts:			30,000
Anna			23,000
Bill			10,000
Cheryl			63,000
		(5,310)	

	Cost £	Accumulated depreciation £	Carrying amount £
Current accounts:		15,415	
Anna			
Bill		4,895	
Cheryl			15,000
			78,000

5

Capital accounts

	Kate £	Hal £	Mary £		Kate £	Hal £	Mary £
				Bal b/d	48,000	38,000	27,000
				Current a/c	6,200		
Goodwill		13,500	13,500	Goodwill	9,000	9,000	9,000
Bank	15,000						
Loan	48,200						
Bal c/d		33,500	22,500				
	63,200	47,000	36,000		63,200	47,000	36,000

Current accounts

	Kate £	Hal £	Mary £		Kate £	Hal £	Mary £
Bal b/d		800		Bal b/d	1,200		2,500
Drawings	20,000	23,500	24,400	Profit	25,000	25,000	25,000
Capital a/c	6,200						
Bal c/d		700	3,100				
	26,200	25,000	27,500		26,200	25,000	27,500

6

Current accounts

	Paul £	Gill £		Paul £	Gill £
Drawings	26,400	18,700	Bal b/d	2,000	2,000
			Profit	20,250	13,500
			Salary		2,500
Bal c/d	1,683	2,217	Profit	5,833	2,917
	28,083	20,917		28,083	20,917

Workings

Profit appropriation

	£
1 Oct to 30 Jun (£45,000 × 9/12)	33,750
Paul (£33,750 × 3/5)	20,250
Gill (£33,750 × 2/5)	13,500
	33,750
1 Jul to 30 Sep (£45,000 × 3/12)	11,250
Paul ((£11,250 – 2,500) × 2/3)	5,833
Gill salary	2,500
Gill profit ((£11,250 – 2,500) × 1/3)	2,917
	11,250

or

	1/10 – 30/6 £	1/7 – 30/9 £	Total £
Profit for distribution	33,750	11,250	45,000
Paul: profit share	20,250	5,833	26,083
Gill: salary		2,500	2,500
Gill: profit share	13,500	2,917	16,417
	33,750	11,250	45,000

CHAPTER 5 Introduction to limited company accounts

1

True	✓
False	

Limited liability means that the owners' liability is limited to the amount that they have paid for their shares.

2 The purpose of financial statements is to provide useful information about the financial performance and financial position of an entity to existing and potential investors, lenders and other creditors (providers of finance). These users are often external to the company and therefore they depend on financial statements for information about a company's performance and position.

Accounting standards and companies legislation ensure that financial statements actually do provide the information that users need to make decisions about providing finance to a company. Without regulation, preparers of financial statements would be able to adopt whatever accounting practices they chose. This would make it impossible for users to compare the financial statements of different entities in any meaningful way. It would also be impossible to compare the financial statements of the same entity over time.

Managers normally wish to show the performance of a company in the best possible light. At worst, without regulation, information might be deliberately presented in such a way as to mislead users.

3

To prepare and approve the annual accounts	
To file the accounts with the Registrar of Companies	
To keep accounting records that are neutral, complete and free from error	✓
To ensure that the accounts show a true and fair view	

The directors have a duty to keep **adequate** accounting records.

4

True	
False	✓

5

Current cost	
Fair value	
Historical cost	
Present value	✓

Synoptic assessment preparation

The questions below are ones to consider once you have completed and passed your assessment. Thinking these questions through will enable you to consider the topics covered in the *Final Accounts Preparation* syllabus in a 'real world' context. This is a vital skill to develop before you attempt the synoptic assessment.

The questions presented are short-form questions. In the real synoptic assessment they will be attached to a wider case study.

Questions

1   **What is the objective of general purpose financial reporting according to the IASB's *Conceptual Framework for Financial Reporting*?**

2   **Give ONE example of a PRIMARY user of general purpose financial reports (financial statements) and explain their need for the information in financial statements.**

3   You have the following information about events on 1 April 20X6.

- A sole trader started business.

- The business was not registered for VAT.

- The sole trader transferred £10,000 of her own money into the business bank account.

- £800 was paid from this account for some office furniture.

- Goods for resale by the business costing £900 were purchased using the trader's personal bank account.

(a) **Complete the capital account as at 1 April 20X6, showing clearly the balance carried down.**

Capital

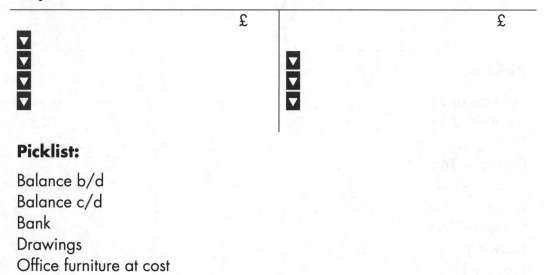

	£		£
▼		▼	
▼		▼	
▼		▼	
▼			

Picklist:

Balance b/d
Balance c/d
Bank
Drawings
Office furniture at cost

Purchases
Purchases ledger control account
Sales
Sales ledger control account
Suspense

At the end of the financial year on 31 March 20X7, you have the following further information:

- Total sales were £66,000.
- Total purchases were £59,120.
- A mark-up of 20% on cost was used throughout the year.

(b) Calculate the value of the cost of goods sold for the year ended 31 March 20X7.

£ ⬚

4 You have the following information about a partnership:

Riva and Sam have been the owners of a partnership business for many years, sharing profits and losses in the ratio 3:2, with Riva receiving the larger share.

On 1 January 20X7, the partnership agreement was changed so that Riva and Sam will share profits and losses in the ratio 2:1, with Riva receiving the larger share.

Goodwill was valued at £72,000 at this date. No entries for goodwill have yet been made in the partnership accounting records.

(a) Show the entries required to introduce the goodwill into the partnership accounting records on 1 January 20X7.

Account name	Amount £	Debit	Credit
▼			
▼			
▼			

Picklist:

Balance b/d
Balance c/d
Bank
Capital – Riva
Capital – Sam
Current – Riva
Current – Sam
Drawings
Goodwill

(b) Which of the following should be included in a partnership agreement? Choose ONE:

The partnership appropriation account ☐

Capital and current accounts for each partner ☐

Salaries and wages to be paid to all employees. ☐

The rate at which interest is to be allowed on capital ☐

Answers

1   The IASB's *Conceptual Framework for Financial Reporting* (2010) states that the objective of general purpose financial reporting is to provide financial information about the reporting entity that is useful to existing and potential investors, lenders and other creditors in making decisions about providing resources to the entity.

2   **Existing and potential investors**

Investors and potential investors need information to help them determine whether they should buy, hold or sell their investment. They need information which helps them to assess the ability of the entity to pay dividends and to assess the potential changes in the market price of their investment.

Alternative example:

Existing and potential lenders and other creditors

Lenders need information that helps them to make decisions about providing or settling loans. They need information which helps them to assess whether their loans and the interest attaching to them will be paid when due.

3   **(a)   Capital**

	£		£
Balance c/d	10,900	Balance b/d	0
		Bank	10,000
		Purchases	900
	10,900		10,900

   (b)   £ | 55,000 |

   £66,000/1.2 = £55,000

4 (a)

Account name	Amount £	Debit	Credit
Goodwill	72,000	✓	
Capital – Riva*	43,200		✓
Capital – Sam**	28,800		✓

*Riva £72,000/5 × 3 = £43,200

**Sam £72,000/5 × 2 = £28,800

(b) The partnership appropriation account ☐

Capital and current accounts for each partner ☐

Salaries and wages to be paid to all employees ☐

The rate at which interest is to be allowed on capital ☑

Glossary of terms

It is useful to be familiar with interchangeable terminology including IFRS and UK GAAP (generally accepted accounting principles).

Below is a short list of the most important terms you are likely to use or come across, together with their international and UK equivalents.

UK term	International term
Profit and loss account	**Statement of profit or loss (or statement of profit or loss and other comprehensive income)**
Turnover or Sales	Revenue or Sales revenue
Operating profit	Profit from operations
Reducing balance depreciation	Diminishing balance depreciation
Depreciation / depreciation expense(s)	Depreciation charge(s)
Balance sheet	**Statement of financial position**
Fixed assets	Non-current assets
Net book value	Carrying amount
Tangible assets	Property, plant and equipment
Stocks	Inventories
Trade debtors or Debtors	Trade receivables
Prepayments	Other receivables
Debtors and prepayments	Trade and other receivables
Cash at bank and in hand	Cash and cash equivalents
Long-term liabilities	Non-current liabilities
Trade creditors or creditors	Trade payables
Accruals	Other payables
Creditors and accruals	Trade and other payables
Capital and reserves	Equity (limited companies)
Profit and loss balance	Retained earnings
Cash flow statement	**Statement of cash flows**

Accountants often have a tendency to use several phrases to describe the same thing! Some of these are listed below:

Different terms for the same thing
Nominal ledger, main ledger or general ledger
Subsidiary ledgers, memorandum ledgers
Subsidiary (sales) ledger, sales ledger
Subsidiary (purchases) ledger, purchases ledger

Bibliography

Association of Accounting Technicians. (2014) *AAT Code of Professional Ethics. Version 2.* [eBook] London, AAT. Available from: https://www.aat.org.uk /sites/default/files/assets/AAT_Code_of_Professional_Ethics.pdf [Accessed 27 April 2016].

International Accounting Standards Board. (2010) Conceptual Framework for Financial Reporting. In *International Financial Reporting Standards* (2010). Retrieved from Deloitte.

International Accounting Standards Board. (2007) IAS 1 Presentation of Financial Statements. In *International Financial Reporting Standards* (2007). Retrieved from Deloitte.

International Accounting Standards Board. (2003) IAS 2 Inventories. In *International Financial Reporting Standards* (2003). Retrieved from Deloitte.

International Accounting Standards Board. (1996) IAS 16 Property, Plant and Equipment. In *International Financial Reporting Standards* (1996). Retrieved from Deloitte.

International Ethics Standards Board for Accountants. (2015) Code of Ethics for Professional Accountants (2015). New York, International Federation of Accountants.

Index

REVIEW FORM

How have you used this Course Book?
(Tick one box only)

☐ Self study

☐ On a course_____

☐ Other _____

Why did you decide to purchase this Course Book? *(Tick one box only)*

☐ Have used BPP materials in the past

☐ Recommendation by friend/colleague

☐ Recommendation by a college lecturer

☐ Saw advertising

☐ Other _____

During the past six months do you recall seeing/receiving either of the following?
(Tick as many boxes as are relevant)

☐ Our advertisement in Accounting Technician

☐ Our Publishing Catalogue

Which (if any) aspects of our advertising do you think are useful?
(Tick as many boxes as are relevant)

☐ Prices and publication dates of new editions

☐ Information on Course Book content

☐ Details of our free online offering

☐ None of the above

Your ratings, comments and suggestions would be appreciated on the following areas of this Course Book.

	Very useful	Useful	Not useful
Chapter overviews	☐	☐	☐
Introductory section	☐	☐	☐
Quality of explanations	☐	☐	☐
Illustrations	☐	☐	☐
Chapter activities	☐	☐	☐
Test your learning	☐	☐	☐
Keywords	☐	☐	☐

	Excellent	Good	Adequate	Poor
Overall opinion of this Course Book	☐	☐	☐	☐

Do you intend to continue using BPP Products?   ☐ Yes ☐ No

Please note any further comments and suggestions/errors on the reverse of this page and return it to: Nisar Ahmed, AAT Head of Programme, BPP Learning Media Ltd, FREEPOST, London, W12 8AA.

Alternatively, the Head of Programme of this edition can be emailed at: nisarahmed@bpp.com

REVIEW FORM (continued)

TELL US WHAT YOU THINK

Please note any further comments and suggestions/errors below